JURISPRUDENCE

SHORT NOTES ;QUICK REVISION BULLET POINTS FOR FIRST YEAR LAW STUDENTS

ADVOCATE SIDDHART BAJPAI

SHORT

NOTES

ON

JURISPRUDENCE

PREFACE

The term 'jurisprudence' is derived from the Latin word *jurisprudentia*', which means the knowledge of the law. If the word *jurisprudentia* is dissected into *Juris* and *prudentia*, *Juris* means law and *prudentia* means skill. There is no such definite definition of jurisprudence. However, various jurists have defined the term jurisprudence. Jeremy Bentham is considered the Father of Jurisprudence. According to him, jurisprudence is a set of philosophical principles and various interpreted theories. This eventually shows us the concept of law. According to Austin, the appropriate subject for jurisprudence is the existing laws or the positive law. He was the first philosopher and jurist who considered jurisprudence as a science. Keeton has defined jurisprudence as the study and systematic arrangements of the general principles of law.

Jurisprudence throws light on the basic principles of law. It shows us the correct path of finding the reason behind the rules of law and understanding their concept. It also helps the judges and lawyers in deriving the proper interpretation of the laws. The study of jurisprudence brings out clarity in understanding the concept of law. It gives a multidimensional approach to the system of law. At times, a huge gap is observed between the law and its application in society. Jurisprudence helps in such cases. It helps in bringing logic to the rules of law so that the application in society can be beneficial for the people. It also shows us the connection of law with subjects such as philosophy, economics, psychology, politics, etc. People, especially judges and lawyers, get a better understanding of the concept of law through the study of jurisprudence. It also helps the authorities to understand how and when any reformation is required. Lord Tennyson, considers jurisprudence as 'the lawless subject of law'.

The origin of jurisprudence is in the Roman civilization. The Romans were quite interested to find out the meaning and the nature of the law. However, at that time the research was quite limited regarding the concept of law. It was also observed that the Greek civilization was also trying to understand the concept of law. Philosophers like Plato, Socrates, Aristotle, etc have given many references regarding the concept of law. With the fall of these civilizations, the Christian States emerged. However, with the emergence of secular States, various new theories came up proposed by John Locke, Rousseau, Blackstone, Hugo, etc, with concepts and evolution of law. During the 17th century, the positive approach towards law saw the light.

Printed by Notion Press Media Pvt Ltd, #7, Red Cross Road,

Egmore, Chennai, Tamil Nadu 600008

First printing edition 2022.

Notion Press Media Pvt Ltd, #7, Red Cross Road,

Egmore, Chennai, Tamil Nadu 600008

Notion Press Media Pvt Ltd, #7, Red Cross Road,

.

CHAPTER 1 JURISPRUDENCE : MEANING & VALUE

Ch.1.1Jurisprudence:Meaning:

Jurisprudence is derived from the Latin terms 'Juris' meaning legal and prudentia meaning "knowledge". It is that science which deals with the **"Knowledge of law"**.

It is defined as a study of the fundamental legal principles including their philosophical, historical and sociological bases, and, an analysis of legal concepts.

It is a type of investigation into the essential principles of law and the legal systems (Salmond). It is the science of the first principles of civil law. The legal concepts like contracts, torts or criminal law consist of a set of rules. It has no such legal authority and further it has no practical application. The jurists have a free approach in their investigations. Further, the method of enquiry in jurisprudence is different from other legal subjects.

The questions answered are: What is law ?

What it is ,for a rule , to be legal rule ? What distinguishes law from morality, etiquette etc.,

The main fields of investigation are the following:

i.   The nature of law, its sources: Administrative of Justice, statutory interpretation etc.,
ii.   An analysis of:

a.   The legal concepts of right and of its kinds and
b.   Concepts like "intention", "negligence" "ownership" "possession" "persons" "liability", "obligations", Substantive and procedural laws" etc.

Ch. 1-2 Value of Jurisprudence:

Jurisprudence does not contain a sets of rules as in contracts or torts and also has no practical application. However, it has its own values, unique and distinctive.

i.   The subject has its own intrinsic interest.
ii.   Its researches have influenced other subjects in the field of political, medical, and social thinking.
iii.   It is educative, as it sharpens the lawyers own techniques.
iv.   Its method and explanations help resolve the complexities of law. Thus, theory helps law to solve problems and,
v.   Professional lawyers may get a glean into the sociology of law i.e., the realities of time, and, make them look-forward with a orientation.

Ch. 1-3 Schools:

There are three main schools of jurisprudence: They are 1. Analytical

2. Historical 3. Ethical Schools.

1.   Analytical School:

Also called English School. It aims at a systematic legal exposition of the various principles. The approach, is dogmatic. The founder of this school is Austin. The school aims at analyzing the contents of the

various legal notions past or present.

Main topics dealt with are:

i.   Analysis of the concept of civil law.
ii.   Analysis of the relationship between systems of law
iii.   Analysis of sovereignty, administration of justice, theory of • legislation, precedents, customs
iv.   An analysis of the concepts -of property, possession, ownership, contracts, trusts, obligations, etc.

1.   Historical School:

The founder of this school is Savigny. It is also called continental school. It aims at examining the general or philosophical part of the legal theory. The approach is historical.

The purpose is to examine the historical evolution or the processes which ultimately lead to legal system. In other words, it examines 'what it is, from what is was'. It deals with the origin and development of those fundamental principles and conceptions so essential in the philosophy of law. These are the same as those dealt with in the analytical school, but the approach is Historical.

The influence of social conditions on legal conceptions is emphsised. It examines now these concepts evolved through generations.

3. Ethical School:

It deals with the general or philosophical part of the science of legislation.

The purpose is to set forth the law, not as it is or has been, but as it ought to be. It does not deal with the present but deals with the ideals for the future.

The theory of Justice in relation to law is the concept of this ethical school. Emphasising the ethical or moral significance of various topics is its main concern.

Grotius is called the father of this school. Kant and Hegel followed him, and developed further the ethical concepts.

In order to understand jurisprudence, as Salmond says, "A study of all the schools is essential because the three schools are closely related and interwoven."

CHAPTER 2 SOURCES OF LAW

Ch.2-1 Sources:

The major sources of law are: i) Legislation, ii) Precedents, iii) Custom.

Ch. 2-2 Legislation: as a superior source: over Precedent:

Salmond opines that 'Case law is gold in the mine, a few grains of the precious metal to the ton of useless matter, while Statute law is the coin of the realm ready lor immediate use'.

Legislation is the main source of law. It consists of the declaration of legal rules by a competent authority like the Parliament or the other legislative bodies. It is an enunciation of principles having the force of law. The courts recognise these as law.

Legislation also called Statute Law has become the standard form of law. The earlier forms, that is precedent, custom based on religious faith or practice or revelations of men have lost much of their efficacy. The result is that legislation is the most powerful and the latest instrument in legal growth.

Advantages or virtues of Legislation: i) Abrogative and Reformative Powers:

The first virtue is its abrogative power. It can abolish an existing law or make a new law. But, a precedent has constitutive efficacy- it is capable of producing very good law. But its operation is irreversible. Once it is stated it stands But, legislation can bring about reforms. Hence, legislation has destructive and reformative power.

i)Efficiency:

The duty of the judiciary is to interpret the law and apply it . The legislature is superior as its duty is to make the law; administrators operate the law. Thus, there is a division in the labour and hence much efficiency.

iii.   Prospective Operation:

Statute declares the law before the commission of any act to which it applies, thus it fulfills the principles of Natural Justice. Law will be known before it is enforced. A judicial precedent creates and declares in

the very act of applying and enforcing it (e.g .Ryland V. Fletcher).

iv.   Law of future:

Legislation can make Acts to meet circumstances not yet arisen.

Precedent requires definite circumstances before the court.

Legislation can fill up any vacancy i.e., settle any doubt that may come to the attention of the legislature. But, a bad precedent remains until another case comes up before the court for solving the doubt or for overruling it.

v.   Superiority in form:

The legislature produces the law in the Statute form i.e. as Acts which are of standard form. Statute law is*brief, clear and easily know-able and accessible. But, case law is hidden deep and buried from sight in the huge records of litigation & Reports.

Hence, case law is like gold that is in the gold mine, hidden in the rocks. But, Statute law is like a coin ready for immediate use.

Salmond appreciates the perfection of the form of Statute Law. Statute Law is authoritative, and it is the duty of the Courts in interpret the words and their true meanings. But, in applying case law, the courts are dealing with the ideas and principles. Statute law is rigid, but case law has the merit that it appeals to reason and justice and hence flexible and adaptation is possible.

Only when the words in the Statute are not clear, that the courts will have to interpret with reference in social purpose.

Ch. 2-3 Precedent:

For the purpose of jurisprudence the sources may be divided into 'legal and historical source's. The legal sources are authoritative, have a right in the courts and have helped the course of legal developments. E.g. The statutes, precedents writings of eminent jurists like Bentham, Austin etc.

The historical sources are not authoritative, cannot have claim as a right in the courts. Precedent therefore is a legal source.

The distinguishing characteristic feature of English law is the judicial precedent. The unwritten law or the common law is purely a product of decided cases, from 13th Century. English judges have contributed considerably for the development of common law.

A judicial precedent speaks in England with authority. It is

not merely evidence of the law but a source of it, and the courts are bound to follow the law that is so established.

Precedent means 'anything said or done furnishing a rule for subsequent conduct'. Judicial decisions speak of truth and hence are followed in later cases. If so followed, such a decision becomes a precedent.

The doctrine of precedent has two meanings. In the first place in a loose meaning, it means that precedents are reported, may be cited and will probably be followed by the courts. In the second i.e. in the strict sense it means that precedents not only have great authority but in certain circumstances they must be followed.

The two theories have many supporters. Sometimes a precedent may be unsatisfactory. The rule so laid down may be be reversed by the Parliament in making the law. Further, the judges have power to reverse their own decisions and correct the mistakes.

Broadly speaking precedents are:

1. Authoritative and 2. Persuasive.

This perhaps is the solution for the controversy between the two theories.

An authoritative precedent is one which judges must follow whether they approve of it or not.

A persuasive precedent is one which the judges are under no obligation to follow, but must take it into consideration and attach such weight as it deserves i.e. it must by itself merit consideration in the eyes of the judges.

Hence, it is true to say that authoritative precedents are legal sources of law but persuasive precedents are historical sources.

1. Authoritative precedent:

The decisions given by the superior courts are the authoritative precedents which must be followed. Hence the decisions of the House of Lords are authoritative in England. In India the decisions of the Supreme Court are binding on all the courts and authorities within the territory of India. (Art.141 Constitution of India). A High Court decision is binding on the lower courts under its jurisdiction in that State.

2. Persuasive precedent:

Persuasive precedents in England are the following:

Foreign decisions e.g. Decisions of U.S. Supreme Court. The decision of other superior courts in the commonwealth countries. Privy council decisions. Judicial dicta.(Means observation stated by the way).

In. India, so far as the Supreme Court is concerned, the decisions of the foreign courts, of the Privy Council and of the U.S. Supreme Courts etc. are persuasive in character. To the High Courts in India, decisions of the Privy Council, U.S. Supreme Court and decisions of other foreign courts are persuasive.

When a precedent is referred to in a court, it is accepted or disregarded. But if it is authoritative, it is binding and should be accepted.

If it is persuasive the court may accept or disregard it.

Disregarding may be of two kinds:

1. It may over-rule it or
2. It may refuse to follow it.

Such a overruled precedent is null and void. The courts of equal authority have no power to over-rule each other's decisions. If two High Courts have given conflicting opinions a legal anomaly is created. This can be resolved only by the Supreme Court.

The meaning of over-ruling is that 'the supposed rule in that decision was not allowed at all. 'Hence the intermediate transactions will be governed by the new rule decided. Overruling is retrospective subject to certain exceptions.

Ch. 2-4 Circumstances which destroy or weaken the binding force of precedents.

1. Abrogation of decisions i.e. over-ruling of decisions.
2. Reversal of a precedent on a different ground.
3. A precedent given in ignorance of the relevant statue.
4. A precedent which his inconsistent with a decision of a High Court or Supreme Court.
5. Precedent sub silentia (not fully argued)
6. Erroneous decisions.

•

1. Abrogation:

This may happen when the legislature makes a statute to negative the precedent. There is abrogation when the higher judicial authority either over-rules or reverses a precedent. There is overruling when the Supreme Court declares that a 'precedent' (of a High Court or Supreme Court) is wrongly decided. E.g. The Supreme Court over-ruled Golaknath's case, in Bharati's case.

The position is that a case cannot be over-ruled by an obiter dictum (said by the way).

Over-ruling may be express or implied. Implied over-ruling is a doctrine of recent origin. In such a circumstances, the earlier case is deprived of its binding authority.

2. Reversal on a different ground.

It may happen that on appeal, a case may be affirmed or reversed on a different ground. This means, that if the appeal is on ground A, the decision of the appellate court may be on ground B. Nothing is said about ground A. This may create some difficulty. According to Salmond, in such cases, the decision is deprived of its absolute binding nature.

3.   Ignorance of Statute.

A decision is not binding if it is given on ignorance of a statute or a subordinate legislation. This was decided by the House of Lords in Young V. Bristol. This is so even if the court knew the existence of a provision in a statute or rule.

Even a lower court may refuse to follow a precedent on such grounds.

4.   Overlooking the decision of higher courts.

If a decision is given by a High Court, overlooking the Supreme Court precedent, then the High Court decision is a bad precedent

5.   Inconsistency among earlier decisions of the same court.

The general rule is that a court is not bound by its own previous decisions if they are conflicting. This may happen when the counsels have not referred to relevant authorities, or it may be that the court has acted in ignorance or forgetfulness of the cases. The binding force of such precedents is weakened. The subsequent court may over-rule the decision.

6.   Precedents sub silentio:

If the decision of the court does not perceive or look to the particular point of law involved, then there is sub silentio. If there are two points of law A & B and decision is given deciding on point A & not on point B(not argued) then there is sub silentio.

The leading case is Gerard V. Worth. If the previous court decides a case without argument, with reference to the point of law, without any citation or authority, such a decision is not binding.

7.   Decisions of equally divided courts:

Where the court is equally divided, in the technical sense there is no decision at all. Hence, such a precedent, has no force at all.

Ch. 2-5 Ratio decidendi :

What the Court decides generally, is the ratio decidendi or rule of law in a case before it. What it decides between the parties to the case, is binding on the parties. The parties under Res Judicata are barred from reopening the case after the final Court of authority makes the decision between them. If A sues B for negligent driving, parties A and B are bound by the decision of the final court.

There are circumstances, when the judgment will be against all the world i.e, in rem. That is it is binding on all third parties. For example, a nullity declaration of a marriage by the Court, determines the status of the parties, but the decision is binding on all.

Development:

The Ratio decidendi or rule of law is produced by the Court in its process of application by the judges. It should have been applied to

the'parties in respect of live issues, argued on both sides. '

In the course of his judgment, the judge may refer to hypothetical situations, or may give his general reasoning. These are therefore not binding. They are called obiter dicta (observations made by the way) and hence, have no binding force. (Blackburn's dicta are exceptions)

The Court declares the ratio, and, applies that to the facts determined by it. Later Courts, may not follow the ratio. They may distinguish or state exceptions to the earlier rule.

For example, in Bridges V. Hawkesworth the plaintiff P found a bundle of currency notes on the floor of the shop of the defendant. The Court applied the principle of "finding is keeping" and held that P was entitled to the notes. However, in S.S. Water Company V.Sharman two golden rings were found by D in the mud pool owned by P. The court, distinguished the earlier case and said, in that case, the notes had been found on the floor of the shop (public place), whereas, in this case, the rings were in the mud owned by P (private place). The Court held that P was entitled/

Difficulty in finding ratio :

It is always not easy to find out what the ratio is in some cases. Cases are there where the Court may not have supplied the reasons. There are other extreme cases, where the decision is too lengthy, and very difficult to find the ratio.

Methods to determine ratio :

Prof. Wambaugh has suggested the "reversal test". This means, we must take the proposition of law (i.e.ratio) & reverse it (i.e., put the opposite of it) and, see whether that would change the decision. If it did, it is a ratio. This test is good but has its own limitations.

The second method is stated by Dr.Goodhart. This is the material facts theory. This means we must ascertain all the relevant facts of the case, as determined by the judge and also look to the decision in respect of them. That is the ratio. This test is more theoretical than practical according to Salmond.

When several separate judgments are given by the judges in a case, the difficulty in finding the ratio is all the more difficult for the Court. In such a case Lord Dunedin says, it is not the Courts duty to find out with great difficulty, the ratio, to be bound by it.

Ch. 2-6 Obiter Dicta :

Means "what is said by the way". This is opposed to ration decidendi.

A ratio decidendi, is a proposition of law or a rule, enunciated by the Court. It should have been applied to the parties, in respect of live issues, and also argued upon in the case. Such a ratio is binding on the later Court. In suitable cases, that court may distinguish the earlier decision. The importance of the "ratio" is that it is binding on the later Court.

However, "obiter" is different. It refers to hypothetical situations or reasoning or circumstances referred to by the judge in his decision. These are generally the observations, made by the judge. The significance is that they are not binding. The Courts will not follow these observations.

It goes to the credit of Blackburn J, for his dicta, in some leading cases, are followed with respect, by the Courts. But, the universal rule is that the obiter dicta are not binding on the later Courts.

Ch. 2-7 Requirements of valid custom:

'CUSTOM' observes Salmond 'is to society what law is to the State'. 'Each is the expression and realisation and the measure of the society's insight. The principles commend themselves to the community Custom embodies them, as acknowledged and approved not by the power of the state but by the public opinion of the society at large'.

A custom may be legal or conventional. Legal Custom has the force of the law is conventional in usage.

The following are the requirements of a valid custom, i)

Immemorial Antiquity :

The local custom should be long standing or of a fixed period which can be determined. Immemorial means beyond the memory of any living person. Hence, the custom must have been observed over a

period, beyond the memory of any living person, i.e., for over 100 years.

ii. Continuity:

The custom must have been enjoyed continuously. If no living man can contradict the custom set up, it must be presumed to be valid.

iii. Enjoyment as of right:

The custom must have been enjoyed as of right. If the custom has only been mentioned or followed by force or by stealth or with license it can have no claim to stand as a right. It must have been followed openly.

iv. Certainty:

The custom must be certain, clear and definite. That which is vague or not impressive will fail.

v. Reasonability:

The custom must be reasonable. This is the most complex and difficult of the requirements of a valid custom. What is reasonable or not is to be decided by the court in accordance with the prevailing notions of natural justice and public morality. Custom must not be either immoral or contrary to public utility.

vi.   Conformity with the general law :

A local custom will not be admitted if it conflicts with the fundamental principles of the law of the land.

vii.   Conformitywithstatutelaw:

The local custom must not conflict with any statute or any rule thereunder. '

viii.   Compatibility with other customs :

It must not be incompatible with other customs within the same locality. The court cannot sanction two hostile rules or customs.

14 ix) Opinio juris sive necessitates :

"Jurists opinion as necessary". The necessary mental element that the custom is obligatory and not merely optional. Such a conviction of mind is obligatory.

Reasons for reception of customary law as law :

1. Custom frequently contains principles of justice and public utility.
2. Backing custom, there is an established usage which is the basis of its continuance for the future.

CHAPTER 3 LEGAL RIGHTS

Ch. 3-1 Legal Rights and Duties :

Rights are concerned with 'interests'. Rights are defined as interests protected by moral or legal rules. But yet rights are different from interests. Interests are things which are to a man's advantage. Eg. He has interest in his freedom or his reputation. If we say that a person has an interest in his reputation, what we mean is, that he stands to advantage of good name in the society, But, if we say that the person has a right to his reputation what we mean is, that others should not take this from him.

Duties:

A duty is an act which one ought to do. Not doing of, amounts to a 'wrong'. A duty may be moral or legal.

It is a legal duty not to sell adulterated milk. If a person is curious, about his neighbours, there is no legal duty not to be so curious, this is a moral duty and therefore cannot be enforced through the courts.

Legal Rights : Characteristics ;

According to Salmond every legal right has the following basic characteristics:

1. It is vested in a person, that person may be called the owner of it, or the subject of it. i.e, the person entitled. E.g. A buys a house from B. A is the owner of the house acquired.
2. It avails against a person. It is on that other person that a corresponding duty is imposed. That person may be called the person bound, or as the person of incidence. E.g. A is the owner of the house. All others are bound by duty not to interfere etc.

3. Right obliges the person bound, to an act or omission in favour of the person entitled. This is the content of the right E.g. others not to interfere with the enjoyment of the house property, by A.
4. The act or omission relates to a thing. It is called as the object or subject matter of the right. E.g. land, house, goods etc.
5. Every legal right has a title. This means certain facts or events by reason of which the right has become vested in the owner E.g. The sale deed executed by vendor B, in favour of A (the vendee). Title vests in A.

A buys goods from B. A becomes the subject or the owner of the

goods so acquired. The person, bound by the duty are the persons in general (against the world i.e., right in Rem).

The content of the right is non-interference with the enjoyment of goods. The object or the subject matter is the house. The title of the right is the conveyance or sale deed by which A has acquired from B.

An ownerless right does not exist and is not recoginsed by law.

Legal rights in a wider sense:

In a wider sense the legal rights do not necessarily correspond with duties. Here a rule of law confers a benefit or advantage over a person. There are four classes of rights.

1. Rights in a strict sense.
2. Liberties.
3. Powers.
4. Immunities.

Each of the above has corresponding :

1. Duties.

2. No rights.
3. abilities.
4. Disabilities.

1. Rights and duties:

Legal right in the 'strict sense' has all the 5 characteristics, and bears a corresponding legal duty. Right to reputation, right to landed property, right to service under a contract etc. These form the bulk of the rights in the legal world, there are corresponding duties on others.

2. Liberties and no rights:

Legal liberty is a benefit which a person derives without legal duty on others. A is at liberty to express his opinions on public affairs. But A has 'no liberty' to publish a defamatory matter. A may defend himself against violence but he has 'no right' to take revenge upon B who has injured him.

3. Powers and liabilities:

The power to make a 'Will, or the power of appointment of an executor. The powers vested in the judges to discharge their functions. These powers have no corresponding duties on others.

But, it may be noted that liability may be correlative of power. e.g. i) An unfaithful spouse may be divorced, ii) Right or power to marry.

iii) Tenant under liability, as tenancy may be terminated by reentry

of owner.

4. Immunities and disabilities:

It is an exemption, i.e., non-subjection e.g. immunity from ordinary criminal courts given to ambassadors. Therefore an immunity creates no disabilities. Disability is the absence of power. He who has no title cannot pass a title. This is a disability of the transferor. A Minor is under a legal disability to be a party to a contract.

Kinds of Legal Rights:

Ch. 3-2 Perfect and Imperfect rights:

A perfect right is one which corresponds to a perfect duty (The duty is recoginsed by law and is enforceable) Eg. Breach of contract. The right is protected and can be enforced by suing for compensation or for specific performance.

Imperfect right is one which is recoginsed by law but is not enforceable. E.g. Time barred debts. Such a right to recover exists but not through the courts.

It may be noted that an imperfect right is a good defense: e.g. when time barred debt is paid by debtor, the creditor may defend his position. An imperfect right may be a sufficient security, E.g. Pledge or mortgage, though the debt is barred still the property remains a security. Further an imperfect right may have the capacity to become perfect eg. acknowledgment of a debt barred by limitation.

Rights against State, are considered imperfect though they are legal rights. In one sense, they are not enforceable against the State, as the State is the strength of it. From lawyer's view, they are enforceable against the State.

Ch. 3-3 Positive and Negative rights:

A positive right corresponds to the positive duty under which the person should do some positive act. A has a right not to be pushed into water, if pushed into water there is a negative duty on others to pull A out of water.

A negative right corresponds to a negative duty; The right gives a benefit; Acts & Omissions belong to this group.

Ch. 3-4 Rights in Rem and right in personam:

Right in rem is a real right available against the world at large. A has

a right in rem to the peaceful enjoyment of his property i.e., no-body should interfere.

Right in personam is a personal right available against a particular person or persons. If A leases out his house his right to receive the rent, is the right against the tenant only. The right of C, a creditor to receive the loan amount from the debtor B, is a right in personam.

Ch. 3-5 Rights in Re-propria and rights in Re-aliena:

Right in re-propria means right over one's own property; title, ownership etc. Right in re-aliena means right of a person over the property of another. Eg. tenants rights encumbrance right etc.

A right in re-aliena is an encumbrance on the property imposing restrictions on the owner. Eg. Mortgage or charlge.

In respect of a right in re-aliena, there is an encumbrance, but the ownership and other rights are vested in the owner.

The right of a tenant or a mortgagee in possession of the property etc. are rights in-aliena. However, the ownership remains with the owner who has the rights in re-propria.

Hence, all encumbrances, are rights in re-aliena: Leases, servitudes, securities and trusts.

In respect of bailor and bailee, the right of the bailee is right in re-aliena but the bailor has rights in re-propria.

CHAPTER 4

LEGAL PERSONALITY

Ch. 4 Personality:

i.   The personality of a human being means the possession of certain characteristics particularly belonging to mankind. E.g.; Power of thought, of speech etc.

Hence, there are certain attributes which make a human being a person having the personality recgnised by law. If these attributes are absent then that human being is not a person at all. E.g. Slaves are like chattels (things) and therefore not persons at all. Conversely, in law there are persons who are not men; e.g., a municipal corporation, A joint stock company etc. are 'persons' though they are not human beings. Similarly an idol is a person.

According to jurisprudential theory a person is any being who is capable of rights and duties. Hence any being who is capable of rights and duties is a person. Persons are the substances. The rights and duties are attributes. This is the juridical significance of personality

which has gained legal recognition capable of rights and duties is a person.

ii.   Persons are of two kinds:

1.   Natural persons.
2.   Legal persons.

A human being is a natural person. Legal persons are beings who are treated for purposes of law as human beings.

In olden days if an ox gored a person to death, the ox was guilty of homicide and it was stoned to death and its flesh not eaten. This is no longer the law to-day. A beast is incapable of legal rights and legal duties. Its interests have no recognition in law. Today if an animal causes hurt to a person, there is no wrong. But the responsibility is no

the owner of the animal. However, cruelty to animals is a criminal offence and to that extent the animal has a legal right. A 'Trust' may be created to benefit a particular class of animals. Eg. Race horses, tigers etc. as beneficiaries. They are entitled to treatment according to the trust dead. However, if the interests of the animal conflict with the interest of human beings, the interest of the human being will prevail.

iii.   Dead Man:

In so far as dead human beings are concerned, the principle is that personality commences on birth and ceases to exist at death. Therefore dead men are not persons in the eye of law. Actually they have laid down their legal personality with their lives. They are destitute of rights and liabilities. They have no rights because they have no interests. A dead man will not continue to be the owner of his property after death. In fact, he is not a owner in the interval between his death and the entry of an executor or an administrator or a successor. But this does not mean that law will ignore the desires and interest of the dead man.

There are three spheres where a man has anxieties after his death.

These are the dead man's body, his reputation and his estate.

Hence law wants to protect such interests.

In respect of the dead body the corpse is the property of nobody. It cannot be disposed of by will; and, wrongful dealing with it will not amount to theft or hurt. But criminal law, secures a dead man, a decent burial and the violation of the dead body or the grave amounts to a criminal offence. Hence the dead man is protected in respect of his body.

A trust for maintenance of a tomb is void. The property is for the use of the living, not of the dead.

Similarly the reputation of the dead is protected under the criminal law of defamation. Libel or slander of the dead is punishable.

In respect of the estate of a dead man, he is allowed to regulate

the action of the successors under a will.

iv.   En vetre as mere:

In respect of unborn persons law does not prevent a man from owning property before he is born. Of course his ownership is contingent because he may not be born at all! Hence, a man may settle property on his wife and unborn persons. Of course, restrictions have been imposed on such powers so as not to arrest property for generations (Transfer of Property Act , Refer Unborn person, perpetuities etc).

A child in the mother's womb is already born for purposes of law. As Justice Coke pointed out, law has conferred certain consideration on the apparent expectation of birth. Thus in respect of property, an unborn child is considered as a child born for the purposes of:

a.   Acquisition of property.
b.   Acquisitions, subject to the law against perpetuities

The problem is not solved whether an unborn person can have a personal and proprietary right. It has been held that a posthumous child is entitled to damages for the-death caused by the defendant. Wilful or negligent injury inflicted on the child which dies after being born alive amounts to murder.

A pregnant woman cannot be condemned and executed to death until the mother is delivered of the child. There is a conflicting decision of the English Court.

Due to the negligence of a Railway company there was a collision. There was a child in a mother's womb which received certain injuries. The court held: That the company was not liable. •

The unborn child has a contingent right and it must be born as a living human being. If the child is born dead the legal personality falls away *ab initio*. If the child dies in the womb or is still-born, his inheritance fails but he gets all the rights even if he is alive for an hour after birth. Law wants to protect the interests of unborn person.

CHAPTER 5 THEORIES OF PUNISHMENT

Ch. 5-1 Theories of punishment and their relative Merits & Demerits:

There is a complexity of social phenomena which is the main cause for commission of crimes. There are certain important social and personal facts which are mainly responsible for crimes.

These are :-

Physical Causes, mental forces, economic causes, political reasons, personal causes etc.

There are many theories concerning the justification of the pun- ishment. As Salmond observes the ends of criminal justice are four in number: Deterrent, Preventive, Reformative and Retribution.

The preventive theory concentrates on the prisoner, but seeks to prevent him, from offending again in the future. The reformative theory sees, in the readjustment of the prisoner to the demand of society as the greatest need of the criminal law. The deterrent theory emphasises the necessity for protecting society, for so punishing the prisoner that he will be barred from breaking the law.

i. Deterrent theory :

The chief end of the law of crime is to make the evil-doer an example & a warning to all persons who are like minded with him. According to this theory offences are the result of conflicts of interests, between that of the wrong-doer and the society. Punishment makes the commission of an offence .an ill bargain for the offender, and debars the potential offender from the commission of crimes. Creation of "fear" in the mind of persons is the essence of this theory.

This theory is criticized as ineffective. During Queen Elizabeth's time, when severe punishment was publicly given to pick pockets, it

was found that other pick pockets were busy in. the crowd which had come to see the punishment!

ii. Preventive theory :

The object of punishment is to prevent repetition of the crime by rendering the offender incapable of again committing the offence. Preventive theory of punishment aims at physical restraint. Prison became an institution because of this theory. In modern times, the disability aspect has been emphasised by statutes conferring power to sentence habitual offenders to preventive terms of imprisonment, penalties, forfeiture or suspension of driving license etc.

Hi) Retributive theory :

This theory is based on "evil for evil". An offence creates an imbalance in the society, and punishment or suffering is the medium through which the balance is restored. It is simply the theory of private vengeance. Revenge is the right of the injured person according to Salmond. It means that a man should be so dealt with as he has done with

others. The basis of this theory is, that evil should be returned for evil. To suffer punishment is to pay a debt due to the law that had been violated. The rule is "A head for a head, a tooth for a tooth and a nail for a nail".

iv. Reformative theory:

The object of this theory is to reclaim the offender, to make him a useful member of the society by bringing about a change in his character and to give a chance to him to lead a free life in Society. According to this theory criminals are generally abnormal persons and the interest of the society is subserved by leaving these persons to the normal law abiding individuals. The stress, here is shifted from crime to the criminal. We must **cure our criminals and not kill them.** E.g. Educational discipline of the criminal.

Corporeal (physical) punishment is deemed to be brutal and degrading both to the offender and to those who inflict it. Preventive

punishment turns the offender into a hard headed criminal. The treatment of the criminal should be humane, his case history should be studied and appropriate measures taken to keep him away from the wrong-doing. Eg. The cases of juvenile offenders First offender's and sex offenders, should be dealt with carefully. Nothing is gained by sending them to the prison to the company of hardened criminals.

Rather they must not be sent to reformative schools which are houses of corrections.

The theory is against all types of corporeal punishment; it commends education, training & proper social moral instructions when in prison. Modern techniques should be used to reform him, to change his attitude and approach to life.

Punishment is not an end itself. It is a means to reform and to rehabilitate the prisoner. Hence, the prisoner should be cured, and not killed.

Conclusion :

Salmond is of the opinion that primary importance is to be given to the deterrent elements is criminal justice. The reformative element should not be over-looked. But neither must be allowed to assume prominence. It is a question of time, place, circumstance and nature of the offence, that should be applied on each case.

CHAPTER 6 PENAL LIABILITY

Ch.6 Liability:

Liability or responsibility is the word or tie that comes into existence as a result of the wrongful act of an individual. This is called Vinculum juris by which a man who is under it, must do certain things. A man's liability consists in these things which he must suffer. It is the ultimatum of the law. It has its sources in the Supreme will of the State. According to Salmond, liability or responsibility is the bond of necessity that exists between the wrong doer, and the remedy. "He who commits a wrong is said to be liable or responsible for it".

Liability may be divided either as civil or criminal or as remedial or penal. In the case of civil or remedial liability, the object of the law is the enforcement of right, whereas in case of criminal or penal liability the purpose is the punishment of the wrong-doer. All criminal liability is penal. Civil liability on the other hand may be either penal or remedial.

Measure of Penal liability : Mens rea:

The basic principle of a liability is embodied in the legal maxim. "**Actus non facit reum nisi mens sit rea**". [The act alone does not amount to guilt, it must be accompanied by a guilty mind, "mens rea"]. Hence, there are **two conditions** to be fulfilled before penal liability can be imposed on a person. It is not enough that a man has done some act. Before the law can justify punishment, an enquiry must be made into the mental attitude of the doer. It is the combination of physical and mental elements that constitutes penal liability. It is not enough to •convict an accused charged of the offence of murder to prove that he has killed another. It should further be proved that he did it intentionally, wilfully and deliberately. According to Salmond, generally a man is penalty responsible for those wrongful acts which he does either wilfully or negligently.

There are three aspects of penal liability viz., conditions, incidence and measure of penal liability. According to Salmond these three elements should be taken into consideration in determining the measure of criminal liability, namely, motive of the offender, the magnitude of the offence, character of the offender. Where there is no inadvertence or negligence, punishment is generally unjustifiable. Hence in inevitable accidents or mistake it is in general a sufficient ground of exemption from penal responsibility.

Ex. A driver knowing fully well, that the bus is not having the breaks, insists to drive the bus; In consequence the bus has gone out of control and has resulted in an accident injuring B.

This is an act committed intentionally and hence the driver is liable for punishment. Here the "Mens Rea" (blame worthy mind) is there. But if the bus has been in good condition as regards breaks system, then while driving, if the accident happens, it could have been said that the accident is inevitable. It has taken place accidentally. Here the driver has no idea of accident but it is due to failure of the breaks the accident has inevitably occurred.

Father was sleeping in a room which was dark and there was a gun kept loaded in that room. His son entered the room, in darkness; the son pressed the trigger of the gun thinking it to be a switch which resulted in firing of the gun resulting in the death of the father. Father was the victim of the bullet but the son had no intention to kill his father. This is inevitable accident not murder.

CHAPTER 7 STANDARD OF CARE

Ch. 7 Negligence:

Negligence is culpable carelessness. That means the absence of such care as it was the duty of the defendant to use. It does not necessarily consist in thoughtlessness or inadvertence. A is guilty of negligence, if he drives furiously into a crowd. A may know that he is exposing others to risk.

Negligence is failure to use sufficient care.

Carelessness may exist to any degree. The degree depends on the risk to which others are exposed. The risk depends on:

1. The magnitude of the threatened evil and
2. The probability of it.

What is the yard stick of care required by Law ?

The answer is mat the "Standard of care" of which nature is capable. 'A' is not liable for the harm ignorantly done by him. This harm he could have avoided with fore-thought. A is liable if he knowingly fails to take steps to stop the harm.

The facts which help to find out the standard required are:

1. The magnitude of the risk.
2. The dangerous form of the activity.

By driving the train at 50 miles per hour, a railway company may cause a fatal accident. But, if the speed is 10 miles per hour perhaps no accident happens. But his saving is done by causing great inconvenience. Hence, the company is not liable.

In professions, want of skill or competence amounts to negligence. The person is expected to use such skill & knowledge, as is necessary for reasonable efficiency. If he is below this, he is negligent and hence liable. An ignorant physician who kills his patient is liable not because he is ignorant, but because being unskillful he ventures to do an act which calls for qualities which he does not possess.

CHAPTER 8

SOLIDITY OBLIGATION

Ch. 8 Obligation:

Obligation is a synonym for duty.

Obligations may mean one class of duties corresponding to rights in personam. E.g.: To collect rent.

Obligation may be vinculum-juris (bond of legal necessity). It binds together two or more individuals. Duty to pay a debt, to perform a contract, to pay damages for torts etc.

Obligation is not merely a duty but it is also a right. Further, an obligation belongs to the group of proprietary rights i.e., the right forms part of the estate of the owner. Therefore, an obligation is defined as a proprietary right in personam or a duty which corresponds to such a right.

"Person entitled" is called a creditor and the person who is bound, is the debtor in a narrow sense. The technical equivalent of an obligation is **choses in action** or thing in action.

E.g.: Debt, a share in a company, claim for damages for tort etc.

The normal type of obligation is between a creditor and a debtor. There may be two or more creditors or debtors, but in such a case, there

may be co-owners or persons jointly bound.

Eg.: 1) Debts by a partnership firm.

2. Debts by principle debtor, guaranteed by one or more sureties.
3. Liability of two or more tort-feasors.-

Hence, the creditor is not obliged to divide his claim into as many different parts as there are debtors. He may recover the entire amount from one debtor and leave that debtor to recover from the co-debtors. If A and B partners of a firm owe Rs.1000 to creditor C,

it does not mean that A and B are under an obligation to pay Rs.500/- each. The debt is single and therefore can be recovered from any person A or B. If the debt is one or single, it is called solidary obligation. That is, each debtor is bound is solidum instead of proparte. (Proportionate

part).

Hence a solidary obligation may be defined as an obligation in

which two or more debtors owe the same things to the same creditor. There are three distinct types: 1. Several 2. Joint and 3. Joint and several.

1. Several: It is several where the thing owed is the same but there are many obligations as there are debtors. Each debtor is bound to the creditor by a distinct and independent Vinculum juris. But the obligation is the same. Hence, performance by one debtor discharges all debtors.
2. Joint: Here, there are two or more debtors but there is only one debt. If one is discharged, all others get discharged.
3. Joint and several: Law treats this for some purposes joint and for other purposes several.

In order to find out the class to which an obligation belongs, it is necessary to find out the origin.

Examples:

1. Several:

Principal debtor and surety-where the suretyship is in a separate agreement. But, if it is in the same agreement it becomes a joint obligation.

2. Joint:

Debts of partners.

3. Joint and several :

(i) Joint tort feasors (ii) Contracts where the obligation is joint and several, i.e., all together & each is individually liable.

The various sources of obligation may be :

1. Contractual.
2. Delictual E.g. Joint tort feasors.
3. Quasi Contractual.
4. In-nominate:

Eg. Obligation of trustee towards beneficiary.

CHAPTER9

PROPERTY

Ch. 9-1 Property:

In its widest sense "property includes all the legal rights of a person of whatever description including thereunder personal as well as proprietary rights. In a narrow sense, property includes the rights of a person and not his personal rights.

Eg.: Land, Chattels, Stocks, Patent rights, Trade marks, Copy rights etc. are property.

Broadly there are two kinds of properties. Corporeal and incorporeal (moveable and immoveable.)

Real and personal come under corporeal. Right in-propria and right in re-aliena come under incoporeal property.

Ch. 9-2 Modes of Acquisition:

1. Occupation or possession:

In case of 'Res nullius' (a thing without an owner) anyone is at liberty to take and keep it and he makes it his own by the very act of taking possession. The possession of the material object is the title to the ownership of it. Possession is the objective realisation of ownership. If a possessory owner is wrongfully deprived of the thing, he can recover it.

A person in possession is deemed to be the owner until and unless proved otherwise. A person in lawful possession cannot be ousted out, even by the owner, without observing the due course of law.

2. Prescription:

It is a mode of acquiring property. May be defined as the effect of lapse of time in creating or destroying rights. It is the operation of time as a vestitive fact. It is of 2 kinds. Positive or aquisitive and negative or extinctive. In the positive prescription it is a title or right; but in negative prescription it is a destructive fact. The rational basis of prescription is the coincidence of possession and ownership of fact and right.

3. Agreement: Includes not merely contracts but all other bilat- eral acts in the law. Agreement is of 2 kinds namely.

1) Assignment and 2) Grants.

By the former existing rights are transferred from one person to another, By the latter new rights are created by way of encumbrance upon

the existing rights of the grantor.

E.g.: Leases:

Agreement is either formal or informal.

4. Inheritance: On the death of the owner heritable rights of deceased survive to the heirs. Personal rights are generally not herit- able. Proprietary rights are usually heritable.

The representative bears the personality of the deceased and has vested in him all the inheritable rights. That is, rights are **vested** in the heir.

Ch. 9-3 Ownership-a bundle of rights:

1. Definition: ownership denotes the relation between a person and an object, forming the subject-matter of ownership(Salmond).

It consist of a bundle of rights, and, all of them are rights in rem-against all the would.

2. The incidence of ownership are :-

i.   **Right of Possession:** The owner has the right to possession of his property. Hence, when this property is hired, pawned, leased, etc the owner has interest in the thing & his right continues, even though he may not be physically in possession.

ii.   **Right of Use :**

The owner has the right to use & to enjoy the property. **(iii) Right to alienate or destroy :-**

The owner has a right to alienate, transfer or to destroy the thing or property as he wishes.

(iv) Duration:

There is no duration for ownership. It is indeterminate.

In cases of lease, bailment, pledge, mortgage etc of property, the duration is for a fixed period.

- But ownership has no such condition. By death of owner, the property conies to his heirs.

v.   **Residuary :-**

This means, even if all the lesser right like lease, easement etc are given away, the residuary will remain with the owner. When these are terminated, they come back to the owner.

Salmond says that it is a fallacy to say the owner's right is "absolute. The reason is the right is subject to the law of the land. The title of the owner is no doubt undisputable, but law may restrict the use of the property.

Ch: 9-4 Kinds of property :-

1.   **Property is mainly** of two kinds: corporeal and incorporeal.

i.   corporeal property is the right of ownership in material things, (visible). It may be movable or immovable. Eg. Land,House, ornaments, gold etc

ii) Incorporeal property : It a proprietary right. It has two divisions.

a.   Encumbrances (Jura in re aliena) like lease, mortgage, servitude, Trust etc.

b.   Jura in re propria- a right over immaterial things: e.g. patent right, trade mark, copy right, Goodwill, etc. Salmond says that the distinction is only theoretical.

2.   Movable & immovable property :

Immovable property (land) (Real property according to English law): has the following elements:

i.   It is a portion on earth's surface.

ii. The ground beneath the surface down to the centre of the earth, and the space above it upto infinity.

iii. All objects under the surface in its natural state i.e. minerals, stones etc.

iv. Building permanent fixtures etc.

Movable property is any corporeal property which is not immovable, e.g. goods, chattels, furniture, etc.

Ch. 9-5 Possession Possession in law & fact :

1. POSSESSION :- It is very difficult to define the concept of "Possession". "Possession is the most basic relation between man & things. (Salmond) It is prima facie evidence of ownership. In fact possession is considered as "nine-points" (out of ten) of law. The meaning is that it is an evidence of ownership, and he who interferes, must prove his better right or title, over the person in possession.

Legal possession should have two elements corpus (physical) & animus (or mental element) to the exclusive use of the thing.

POSSESSION in fact :-

'It is a relationship between a person and a thing" (Salmond)

To possess means to have physical control. Such a control is relative i.e., (1) it may be absolute e.g. a ring a person wears; (2) it may be to exclude other persons from interfering i.e., to keep a thing is a safe.

Two conditions are essential: (i) corpus i.e., to use the thing possessed and (ii) Animus (intention) to use it to oneself exclusively.

Hence, what is required is that the person should have a general control over the thing & should be capable of using it, excluding others. Then there is "possession in fact".

Possession in Law :-

Law given protection to possession. The person in possession has a right in rem. When he is wrongfully dispossessed, the court first determines whether the plaintiff was in possession, and, if so he is protected. If A takes away B's watch, law gives possessory remedy to B.

Legal possession is different from physical possession. A's guests at dinner are provided with spoons, forks etc, Guest has physical possession, he is not entitled to take away the spoons.

Court generally decides in case of dispute, who had the better title. In **Bridges V Hawksworth,** a bundle of currency notes, was found by a customer C, on the floor shop of A. The owner could not not be traced. Held, Q.the finder was entitled...

In **Armory V Delamorie,** the Chimney sweeper C found a golden ring when he was sweeping. He gave it to B Goldsmith's servant for valuation. B refused to return. Held C had a better title.

Possession in law or legal possession should have corpus and animus. Corpus means effective control over the thing & to exclude others. Animus is intention to have it as owner. However a child with a coin in its hand, may not have power to exclude others, but still it has legal possession.

Possession is law is possible without knowledge. A may have a golden ring in his well; he may not know it. If 'C' finds it, 'A' is entitled as he has legal possession (Sharman's case).

Ch. 9-6 Possession and ownership distinguished: Possession Ownership

1. Possession is the most 1. ownership denotes the relation basic relation between man between a person and an object form and things. ing the subject matter of ownership.

2The concept is complex 2. The incidents of ownership, are

possession may not be legal, but

still it is his possession

3. The duration of possession is generally temporary.

4. Deals with a factual relationship only.
5. Possession may be legal, non-legal & even a

pre-legal concept.

definite.

Right to possession, to use, to enjoy, to

alienate, or to destroy the thing, are

exclusive to the owner. The owner has title vested in him.

3 The duration is permanent

4. Deals with legal relationship in a system of law.
5. It is a legal concept in its strict sense.

i

Ch. 9-7 Vested & Contingent Ownership:

Ownership may be Vested or contingent. T executes his will giving his property to his wife W for life and on her death to A, (if A is alive on her death) or to B.

Here A & B have a contingent ownership ie., A should be alive on the death of W, B gets ownership if A is not alive on W's death. Hence, vested ownership is absolute, but contingent ownership is conditional.

Vested Contingent.

1. Owner's title is perfect. 1. On fulfilment of some

condition the ownership

.*

2. Owns property absolutely.

3. Investitive fact is complete
4. Title is complete by itself

becomes perfect.

2. Owns property conditionally

3. It is incomplete.
4. It is something more than mere chance or possibility;

There is

incomplete title.

Ch. 9-8 : Real and Personal Property:

These are English concepts and "Real refers to immovable property; "personal property" refers to movables (Refer Ch.9.4)

Ch. 9-9 Legal & equitable Ownership :

Legal ownership originated from English common law; but equitable ownership is traceable to Equity and chancery, courts. Though law & equity courts were fused together, the distinction between legal and equitable ownership, still continues.

If A orally assigns a debt to B. A remains a legal owner, but B becomes an equitable owner. The debt is one, but has two owners.

This is so in case of equitable mortgage. Legal ownership is different from this, though the property is the same. In fact, there will be legal ownership (of owner) in all equitable mortgages made by him.

Ch. 9-10 Corporeal & Incorporeal Ownership :

Corporeal refers to Land, house, machinery etc material objects (tangible) But incorporeal refers to copyright, patent, trade mark, goodwill of business, right of way etc (Intangibles).

If A has Rs.10,000/- with him, it is corporeal ownership If A owes Rs.10,000/- to B, the right of B to recover , is incorporeal. , Add Ch. 9.4

Ch.9-11 Trust & Beneficial Ownership :

In case of a trust, the trustee is vested with ownership of the trust property; But, the beneficiary has the beneficial ownership. Trustee's ownership is one of form, than of substance; it is nominal. He should use his ownership for the benefit of the beneficiary.

It was to protect the interests of the beneficiary (called **cestui que trust)** that the Chancery court recognised the trust under equity law. Trustee should use the property for the benefit of the beneficiary only., and, not for his own use. If he misuses, he becomes liable to the beneficiary.

Ch. 9-12. Sole & Co-ownerships :

The general rule is that there could be one owner only ie., sole owner for a property. Two or more persons may have vested ownership in the same property, e.g. partners are co-owners of the partnership property. Co-ownership may be either ownership-in-common and joint-ownership. On the death of a co-owner, in ownership-in-common,

his right vests in his heirs according to the Law of inheritance. On the death of a Joint-owner, the right vests by survivorship.

CHAPTER 10 MISCELLANEOUS

Ch.10-1 Jus Necessitatis:

Necessity knows no law. (Necessitatis non habet legem). In the theory of wilful wrong doing, motive of "necessity" operates as an excuse, in some circumstances and it is called Jus necesitatis.

i.   Necessity is not the inevitable thing where there is no choice at all. In necessity there are choices and the person selects under compelling reasons, the one for the other. Hence there is choice of values. In order to save life, one may damage the property of another: one may pull down a thatchet in order to save the others from the spreading of fire.
ii.   Further, necessity creates a motive in him and in fulfilling it, the person will not be afraid of punishment. Two drowning persons A and B cling to a plank which is not in a position to support more than one. A may be under a moral duty to sacrifice to save B. But if A pulls

  • away and saves his own life, he is protected under self preservation.

Similarly two shipwrecked sailors were forced to starve for several days and then to kill a boy and eat him to save themselves. The act of killing may be murder, but it is done under extreme necessity. Necessity is a legal defence. The sailors of course are guilty of murder. But, the court reduced the punishment taking into consideration the circumstances of necessity. (R. Vs. Dudley)

Ch.10-2 Possessory remedies:

Possessions is a good title of right against any one who cannot show a better title. If a wrong doer is in possession, he is having a good title against all except the real owner. The real owner must proceed according to law, to recover, the same. The intention of law is that every person in possession is entitled, until he is deprived of itaccording to the decision of the court. Hence, for the protection of the possessor, certain remedies are provided which are called 'possessory remedies'.

Armory Vs. Delamarie is the leading case.

The reasons for providing such remedies are three:

i.   Imperfection of early remedies: The procedure by which the owner recovered was cumbersome, dilatory and inefficient. There were many pit-falls also. Hence, it was considered that "Possession was nine points of law". Hence the original state of affairs must first be restored. Hence, possession must be given to him who had it first. Then, the question of title was to be dealt with by the court.
ii. The difficulty of the proof of ownership is the second reason a) Prior possession is prima facie proof of title, b) The defendant is always at liberty to show that he has a better title, c) The defendant who has violated the possession is not allowed to set up the plea of jus terti (third party's right of ownership).
iii. The third reason is the evil of violent self-help. Under this a person may take advantage over another. A may, by force seize the property from B. B is to be protected and the possessory remedies are necessary for him.

Ch. 10-3 Vestitive facts: (Title):

Every right is a source of that from which it flows. This source is a fact, By birth a child gets certain rights. Birth is a fact. By purchase, a vendee gets a right. Here, purchaser is a fact. Hence the fact is the root from which the right proceeds. Such a source or title may be original or derivative. In catching a fish by fisherman A, the original title is acquired by A. If A sells the fish to B, B gets the derivative title. A's title is lost. That is, it is extinctive.

Hence vestitive Facts =

1. Investitive Fact = Original or derivative = Create Rights
2. Divestitive Fact = Extinctive facts = Destroy Rights

3. Derivative or alienative facts = Transfer of Rights

Hence, A's title to fish is a investitive fact. His transfer of it to B, makes it a divestitive fact. Hence, these investitive and divestive facts are called vestitive facts. The right of the creditor to receive his debt-amount becomes extinct when payment is received by him. This extintive fact is also a vestitive fact.

Hence, vestitive facts include the creation, transfer and extinction of a right. These may operate voluntarily or may be involuntary.

Ch. 10-4 Quasi-Contract Obligations:

Obligations are of four kinds:

1. Contractual.

2.

Delictual or tortious.
3. Quasi-Contractual and
4. Innominate.

Obligation arising from quasi contract:

These are obligations which are not in the true sense contractual, but which the law treats as if there were such obligations. Roman Law called them quasi res extra contracts & English Law called them Implied or Quasi-contracts. A quasi contract arises from a contract implied in law. If A entres a bus, he has impliedly agreed to pay the fare. This is implied contract, but not a quasi contract. Quasi contract obligation is of two kinds:

i. A debt is a contractual obligation. But a judgement-debtor is under a quasi contract.

If A obtains money from B by fraudulent misrepresentation B may sue in tort for deceit or on a ficitious contract for the return of the money.

Reasons for recognising quasi-contracts:

i. The traditional classification of the various actions into contract or tort
ii. There is a desire to supply a theoretical base for new forms of obligations.

iii. There is a desire of plaintiff to obtain superior efficiency of contractual remedies.

Quasi-contracts are dealt with in Sns.68 to 72 of the Contract Act.

Ch.10-5 Servitude: (Easementary right)

It is an encumbrance which conditions the right of the claimant-owner to the limited use of the servient tenement without the possession of it, or ownership.

Eg. A right of way, right to air and light etc. Servitudes are of two kinds.

•

i) Private ii) Public.

A Private servitude is one which is vested in a determinate individual e.g. right of way, right to fishing public servitude is vested in the public at large, as in customary easement i.e., to bury the dead at a particular place.

According to Salmond a servitude is a right to a limited use of land, unaccompained by ownership. It is a right in rem.

Servitude exists as a right over immovable property only.

Ch. 10-6 Rebuttable presumptions:

Presumptions are inferences drawn from the experience of mankind. That is, from a set of known circumstances, the unknown is presumed. The main function of presumption, is to allow the court to draw inference from proved or known facts, about unknown facts. The court presumes at the first instance the existence of certain facts. Sn.118 of Negotiable Instruments-Act provides certain presumptions. Similarly the evidence Act.

The date and signature, consideration, endorsements etc., of a N/I are presumed to be correct until the contrary is proved. When proved the presumption becomes rebutted. (Add Evidence Act: Presumption).

Ch. 10-7 Animus possidendi:

The essential element to constitute possession is "Animus possidendi". That is , an intention and this is essential. If there is corpus (physical detention of property), in addition to animus, it becomes juristic possession. The special feature is, the possession must be an exclusive claim. The claim need not be absolute. A bailee or mortgagee is entitled to juristic possession though he cannot exclude the real owner.

Animus possidendi need not be a claim on his own behalf. A person may possess a thing on his own account or on account of another.

Eg. Agent, Servant, a trustee etc

Ch.10-8 Mediate and immediate possession:

A person may possess a thing for and on account of some one else. This is called "mediate possession". If a person acquires directly or personally it is immediate possession. A sends B to buy goods for A. The moment B buys the goods, A gets the mediate possession of the goods, B gets immediate possession.

Mediate possession is of 3 kinds, i) Acquired through agent or servant, ii) Acquired through a borrower or tenant, iii) Acquired through a pawnee. Leading cases: 1. Hague Vs. West.

2. Marvin Vs. Mallace.

A bought a horse from B. He lent it to B, for a month. Held: The horse had been delivered. Hence, B holds as bailee.

In mediate possession the persons are in possession of the same thing at the same time. One is having the immediate possession whereas the other mediate possession.

Eg. Land-Lord and tenant, Principal and agent.

Ch. 10-9 Mischief Rule:

The primary duty of the courts is to "interpret" the Law.

The principle of Interpretation of Statutes styled "Mischief Rule" was enuciated in Heydon's case. In 1584 the Barons of exchequer said, that, for a true interpretation of a statute, four items should be considered:

1. What was the common law before the making of the Act?
2. What was the mischief and defect for which the common law did not provide ?
3. What remedy the Parliament has provided ?
4. The true reason of the remedy.

Since then this rule of contruction is followed by the courts as it is a safe guide to the problems of Interpretation.

Smith Vs. Hughes : The prostitutes were attracting the attention of the passers-by. The street Offences Act was made which provided for punishment for soliciting "In the street". The prostitutes attracted the people from their balconies and windows, and not in the streets.

Held as the mischief was the solicitation of people, by the pros- titutes, the Act had made a remedy for it, i.e., to clean the roads. The court held that solicitation from the balcony was "In the Street" and hence the prostitutes, were punishable.

The judges have interpreted in such a manner as to supress the mischief "In the Street", and, to advance the remedy, that is, to clean the streets.

Under this concept the judges may prevent any evasions and any continuance of the mischief. It is, within their province to add force and life to cure and to provide a remedy according to the true

intentions of the Parliament. This intention is to be inferred from the natural and plain meaning of statute itself.

Ch. 10-10 Constitutional Law :

The fundamental or the essential elements containing the details of States structure and State action, constitute constitutional law. In fact, Constitutional law is a body of those legal rules which determine the Constitution of the State. It is the Organic law of the State. The more fundamental and far reaching principles come under the constitution.

It contains the structure of the legislature, the methods of its actions, the structure and operation of subordinate legislatures like the local States. But structure of Municipality etc. is not part of the constitution.

The Organisation, powers and jurisdiction of the Supreme Court come within the Constitution. Other courts may not find a place there.

The organisation, power and functions of the Executive Head come within the Constitution.

A Constitution is rigid when it is written as in the U.S., India etc. It is flexible when unwritten as in England.

The Constitutional Practices customs and conventions are as a matter of fact prior to Constitutional law.

Salmond says that Constitutional law is a judicial theory. Here law and fact may be different. De facto and de jure powers may be in different persons or authorities (e.g. Crown's or Indian Presidents powers). It contains a charter of rights called fundamental.

These discrepancies in fact and in law are there in every constitution. The will of the body politic as expressed through the legislature and the courts may express itself and determine the Constitutional fact or theory

It consists of those rules which govern Sovereign States in their relations and conduct towards each other. To some, international law is a branch of Natural Law or rules of Natural Justice; to others it is a kind of Customary law or of a kind of imperative law enforced by international opinion. It may be a kind of Conventional law having its source in International custom.

There is nothing wrong to think that International law belongs to each of the 4 different laws: Natural law, Customary law, Imperative law and Conventional law. Though consent is the basis, it is not fully so. In respect of a new State, the rules become applicable to it. On the other hand, even in respect of big States, it may be correct to say that these have agreed through their representatives to all the rules of the law of the Nations.

There is a broad division of International Law into Common Law of Nations and particular principles of law of Nations. Universally acknowledged fundamental principles of International Law belong to the first but those between two or more States to the second.

Whether International law, is law, is a controversy. Positivists say it cannot be called law proper, as it has no law making body & also has no sanction. Some refer to natural law to show its binding force. Others say consent of states is the basis. The truth is between these two.

It may not have all features of standard legal system of law-making, courts with compulsory jurisdiction, and law enforcement system, but it **is more than** a species of morality. It falls short of a rigid definition of law.

CHAPTER11 NATURE OF LAW

Ch. 11-1 The function & purpose of Law :

Law is a means to an end and not an end in itself. The aim of law is to secure *justice*. Law is a body of principles recognised and applied by the State in the administration of Justice. Jurisprudence deals with the concept of justice.

i. Justice means 'equal treatment to all, placed alike'. Racial segregation law is against this concept, and, hence according to naturalists, it is no law at all. Of course there may be classifications which are legally valid.
ii. Justice may be (a) distributive and (b) corrective.

It is "distributive" when it brings about social equilibrium. It demands equal treatment when persons are similarly placed. Barring blue-eyed persons from voting, is a clear violation of equality clause. Parliament or Legislature may make law guaranteeing and defining equality.

A person's right to enjoy his property may be upset by constant trespass by his neighbour. In such a case "corrective justice" helps to get compensation from such a trespasser. Courts and tribunals administer this corrective justice. In so doing, they apply a large number of rules: giving opportunity to both sides a fair hearing, barring interested judge from presiding etc. The objective is to provide equal protection to all who are placed in equal position.

One happy result of 'corrective justice' of the court is that it has brought about continuity. This means, on the experience of the past, the public may ascertain what the result would be.

Social Engineering:

The above analysis has referred to individual rights, but, when

we look to the interests of the individuals in society as a whole, their rights and their conflicting social interests, we find law playing the role of "social engineering". This aims at maximum fulfilment of the interests of the community and of its members and also to promote the smooth running of the machinery or the society. The architect of this is **Roscoe Pound.**

Law should be just, but more than that it should be uniform definite certain, known and permanent. This enables a person, to predict what he may get from the courts.

Impartiality is the objective of law; publicly declared principles protect the administration of justice.

People in Society need not be at the mercy of others. Hence the saying "rule of law is always preferable to rule of men".

Law assures stability and security of social order.

Demerits:

i.   Law suffers from rigidity.
ii.   It may not change to social needs by changing itself. Thus, it lags behind social changes.
iii.   Law is becoming more complex. To meet competing interests more laws are continuously passed often changed and the citizens may not know where they stand.

Ch. 11-2 Questions of law & Questions of Fact.

Questions which come up for determination before the courts are "questions of fact" and "questions of law".

a.   Question of law: •

It is used in three different senses.

i.   Where the court is bound to answer a question in accordance with a rule of law,-(not in its own estimation)- it is deciding a question of law. A child below 7 years of age cannot be criminally liable. This is determined according to I.P.C. Sn.82.

ii.   It means, a question as to what is the law to be applied in a particular case. The rule may be unsettled or ambiguous or not yet determined so far. Once it is determined it becomes authoritative. This is

followed in later cases.

iii.   Questions of law are decided by judges and questions of facts by the jury, (in England) But, there are many circumstances, where the courts decide questions of fact.

b.   Questions of fact bears three meanings:

i.   A question not predetermined by any rule of law.
ii.   It covers all question excepts what the law is.
iii.   Those questions which are to be answered by the jury.

c.   Judicial discreation and judicial opinion:

Besides these two, i.e., questions of law and of fact there is the judicial determination based on judicial discretion. Further there is the smaller field where judicial opinion will have its role to play.

eg. i) Whether 'A' has committed an offence, is a question of fact, decided on proved facts.

ii.   What particular offence is committed, is determined in relation to the ingredients of the offences. This is a question of law.

iii.   What punishment is to be awarded, is a "judicial discretion".
iv.   In a civil case, for example, whether the defendant was driving with 'due care and caution', is determined by judicial opinion.

d.   Presumption and legal fiction:

v.   Questions of facts into questions of law: This transformation is possible in case of presumptions, (rebuttable or irrebuttable)Based on facts, a presumption of law is made.
vi.   In the case of legal fictions, there is a departure from facts to a fiction of law: An adopted son, is by fiction, the son of the adoptive father, and has all the rights according to law.

Thus, all questions are either questions of law or questions fact is, only a general rule. In the above analysis, it is clear that judicial discretion, judicial opinions, presumptions and legal fictions have their own role to play in the administration of justice.

Ch. 11-3 Substantive law and Procedural law: 1.

DefinitionandDifferences:

Substantive law defines the rights, while procedural determines the remedies. This suggestion is true in theory, but has limited scope in practice.

Many legal rights eg. to. go in appeal to higher courts, to

cross-examine a witness, are rights in the procedural laws. Many remedies

e.g. levy of fines, imposition of punishment are substantive law i.e., The Indian Penal Code. Hence, it is not correct to say that procedural law deals with remedies only.

Substantive Law

1. This refers to the purpose and the subject matter but does not concern itself with the process.

Procedural Law

This governs the process of litigation i.e., actions. These include all the legal proceeding Civil & Criminal i.e.Summons, Pleading, Proof, Judgment, Execution.

2. This concerns itself with the This deals with the means of

ends of Justice.

3. It deals with the matters litigated.

reaching the ends.

3. It regulates the conduct of

the courts, the litigants and their relations.(eg. Cr.P.C.,C.P.C.)

4. What facts constitute a wrong is substantive.
5. Substantive law defines the

legal rights.

4. What constitutes' proof of wrong is procedural.
5. Procedures define the modes &

conditions of the application of remedy.

Ch.11-5: Civil & Criminal Justice :

Lex Civil includes both civil and criminal law. But they are different. Blackstone divided wrongs into private wrongs & public wrongs.

1. Infringement of a person's civil right was a civil injury. Violations of public rights & duties (affecting the community) were crimes.
2. Remedy :- Individuals seek damages etc in Civil matters, But, State punishes in criminal matter.
3. Initiation :- Individual brings action in Civil matters in his name. But State is the injured party in Crimes and it procures in its name through officials.
4. Courts:- Civil wrongs are tried in civil courts but offences are tried in criminal courts.

Evidence to be produced is different in these courts; Even in appeal the nature of evidence is different.

5. Civil courts award damages, injunction, specific performances, money decree etc.

Criminal courts visit punishment, death penalty, Imprisonment, fine, release on probation etc.

Though these differences are maintained still there are overlappings Wrongs against state are offenses but violation of contract with Govt non-payment of tax etc are civil matters.

There are acts like trespass, defamation which are both civil & criminal There are instancee wherein compensation is awarded to the aggrieved party for criminal matters.

Conclusion :- Even though these overlappings are there, no one can doubt that the objects, methods of enforcement, evidence, & proceedings & impact in civil & Criminal matters are distinctly different.

Ch.11-6 Secondary Functions of Courts :

The primary function of courts, in the administration of justice, is upholding the rights, providing remedies (Civil courts) and, punishment (criminal courts)

However, administration of Justice in its wider sense also includes various secondary functions of courts

These functions are :

a. Action against the state :

Citizen may sue the State to recover dues from it & for restitution of property detained by it. There are the proceedings and there is no coercion or constraint by the State in which the Judiciary itself is a part.

b. Declaration of Right:

A party may claim for a declaration if his rights are under "cloud", e.g. Declaration of Legitimacy, Status as adopted son, executor, elected member etc (sn.34. Specific Relief Act)

c. Administration :

7

Courts undertake the responsibility like administration of estate, or, distribution of property, liquidation of a company, trust administration etc.

d. Titles or Rights :

Judicial decrees may create certain rights or extinguish certain rights. Decree of divorce, judicial separation, removal of trustee, appointing administrator etc.

Thus the scope of civil" courts is extensive to include these secondary functions.

MAJOR THEORIES OF LAW

Ch. 12-1 Major Theories:

The major theories of law, which are prominent in legal theory (jurisprudence) are the following:

   i. Law as the dictate of Reason. This is the natural law theory.
  ii. Law as the command of the Sovereign of the State. This is the imperative theory. (Austin's theory)
  iii. Law as the practice of courts. This is the theory of "Legal Realism". (Salmond's theory)
  iv. Law as a system of Rules. This is called as Hart's theory. **Ch.12-1 Natural Law theory:**

Natural law theory defines "law as the dictate of reason". The theorists are called the Naturalists.

Law consists of principles of Justice and morality which are deduced from the objective moral principles of nature. These are rules of conduct for human beings, and, may be discovered by natural reason and commonsense. These are true law and are not obligatory but are followed naturally by the people. This is the essence of this theory of law.

Naturalists oppose the positive law founded in Codes, Statutes, Constitutions etc., These are obligatory and are enforced by force All these, which are opposed to natural law, are riot really true law, but are only a violation or abuse of law.

Merits:

The merits of this theory of law are as follows:

i. Superior standard:

When the ordinary positive law falls short of some ideal, the people appeal to some higher standard based on natural law. The cry of the people in such cases would be "an unjust law is no law at all". Thus natural law has some leading role to play.

ii. Obedience:

The phenomena of nature like the movement of the moon, the earth and the heavenly bodies are governed by the law of nature obligatory and are being followed. However, people have made their own customs, manners, fashions etc., and these are arbitrary and conventional. They do not command obedience as natural law.

iii. Stoic's Philosophy:

The Stoic philosophers developed this concept further. According to them, "man should live, according to nature" since, man by
iv.   nature is endowed with reason. True law is equal to right reasoning.

Natural Rights:

On the ground of "reasoning", the fundamental human rights have their base in natural law. For example, equality, has its base in natural law Naturalists say

"Adwarfisasmuchaman,asagiantis".

Criticism:

Natural law has its own formidable difficulties, i)

Not followed in Practice:

Natural law holds that the people 'ought' to follow its rules. But, in reality this may not be so. For example, man out to beget children, just like a tree bearing fruits. This may not be followed. Even States may impose restrictions on begetting children.

ii. Fulfilling functions:

The principle of nature is that everything has its proper function and so, it must fulfill this function. The function of a watch is to show correct-time, as per its maker. This is its definite purpose. This

analogy is not fully applicable to man. His purposes and functions are varied. The question about his maker god creates many other problems.

iii. Functions:

According to nature, it is the function of smoke to rise, fire to burn, of tree to bear fruits, and of wind to blow. Likewise there are many functions of man founded on "reason".

iv. There is no acceptance of natural law, universally. Slavery was recognised in Rome and Greece. Inequality prevails on the basis of religion, colour etc.
v. Contents:

The contents of natural law are also changing. Monogamy is recoginsed in many States ; Polygamy is some others etc.

vi. Natural law has not provided for the security and protection of property and of the person of the individuals.
vii. Disputes are solved or decided by the Courts and tribunals. Applying moral or natural law, it may become difficult for them to solve.

Ch. 12-2 Imperative Theory : Austin

Imperative theory of law defines "law as the command of the

sovereign"

This theory states what a legal rule is, and, distinguishes it from a 'just rule' or 'a moral rule'. It takes into consideration the formal criteria of a legal rule, and distinguishes it from morals, etiquette etc.

Trieste is founder of this theory is. Austin. According to him positive law has three characteristic features : .

i. It is a type of command;
ii. It is laid down by the political sovereign &
iii. It is enforced by a sanction.

i. Commands:

According to Austin, every positive law is a direct or circuitous command of the monarch or the sovereign, to his subjects.

Austin explains the nature of these commands. In a State, where there is an absolute Ruler, by name R, are all the orders made by him commands? His order to his servants to close the door, or to arrange for a banquet; (if not followed the servant may be punished). There are not commands but only desires according to Austin. To be law, the command must be a general command. Of course, generality alone is not sufficient to be a law.

ii. Political Sovereign:

Law emanates from the political Sovereign or Superior. A sovereign may be a person or a group of persons, but not obedient to any other person. He enjoys the obedience of his subjects; Of course, perfect obedience may not be available. Laws may be obeyed out of respect, fear, habit or wisdom. The reason is not important for Austin, but, obedience to the sovereign exists as a fact, in general.

iii. Sanction:

Human nature being what it is, a sovereign without a means to enforce his commands would have no scope. Law stands in need of sanctions. To Austin law is something for the citizen to obey, not as he pleases but whether he likes it or not. This can be achieved by using some coercion (force), that is, by inflicting punishment, by the sovereign. Thus, sanction is part of law.

Criticism:

Austin's theory has been attacked by many.

i. The Naturalists, opposed the positive law, stating that Codes, Statutes, Constitutions etc. are enforced by force and, hence, are not true law, but a violation of law.

Moral and ethical base is essential for a good law and there cannot be good positive law, without this base.

ii.   Austin's definition of law as a command of the sovereign, is silent about customary law. Viewed from this angle, international law is no, law all according to Austin. In reality this is not so.

iii.   There are some laws which are not commands, Sbut are rules which confer only powers. Right to vote, right to contest for election etc. examples.

iv.   Laws continue even after the extinction of the actual law giver. Some provisions of the Constitutions provide for restrictions on the law giver and some provisions cannot be changed, in some States, e.g. basic structure in India.

v.   English law is full of judge-made law. Austinians argue that judges are the delegates of the Parliament. But, this is not so in reality. Under judicial review in many States judges declare law as null and void. Hence Austin's Theory is inadequate to explain this.

vi.   Rules defining sovereignty are varied. Modern States have written Constitutions. These provisions are hardly the commands of the sovereign.

Conclusions:

Though critics have an edge against the imperative theory, the fact remains, that this theory contains a lot of truth.

The law emanates from and is visited with penalty by an authority.

This is best explained by imperative theory than by any other theory.

Ch. 12-3 Law as the practice of Courts. Salmond

Salmond's definition of law (legal realism).

Law. is the expression of the will of the State, through the Legislature (sovereign) (Positivists' theory). Legal realism takes the position that the will of the State, is one that is expressed through the medium of the courts. The shift is from the sovereign to the Court. To the realist, the sovereign is the court.

Salmond as a legal realist, stated that all law is not made by the legislature, but courts do make law. But, in reality all law, however made, (Legislation, custom, judicial precedent) is recognised and administered by the Courts. Further, those which are not rules are not followed. Hence, he emphasises that in order to know the true law, we must look to the Courts, and not to the legislature.

On the above analysis, Salmond defined law. "It is the body of principles recognised and applied by the State in the administration of

Justice, as the rules recognised and acted on by the Courts of Justice.

Criticism :

i.   AgenciesotherthanCourts :

There are in the modern State, many other agencies, other than law courts to recognise and to apply the law. The Tribunals and the quasi-judicial bodies belong to this category. The House of Commands has exclusive powers to recognise and to punish for violation of its privileges.

ii. Exclusion of statute law :

Critics hold the view, that Salmond's definition applies to case-law and not to statute law. The reason is, a statute becomes operative, as soon as it is made and, need not wait for recognition by the Courts. To this Salmond answers : when the Courts and the Legislature are working in harmony, it does not matter whether the statute law is law because Courts recognise it, or, Courts apply because it is a statute made by Legislature. The truth is the same. (Of course problems arise when a law is struck down by the courts as.null and void).

iii. Holmes's theory :

A strong supporter of legal realism is Holmes. To him "all law is in reality judge-made." Taking the case of a "bad man", who is interested in securing his selfish interest, he says such a person looks to the Courts to know what they would do. In reality the Courts guided

by judicial discretion interpret the law and decide. Hence, it is for the courts to say what the statute means. From this angle : **the courts put life into the dead words of the statute.** Further questions of law are decided by reference and deductions of the Statute. Hence, Holmes says **"the life of the law has not been logic, it has been experience "**. Hence, the position is that a statement of law is a prediction of what the courts will decide.

Criticism :

1. Affects definitions:

According to this theory, no one could ever say. what the law is; but he could only predict what the judges might do. However, this affects the "definiteness" of law, and, in reality this is not he position.

2. Legislature makes law :

A statute is operative as soon as it is made, it need not wait for the recognition by the Courts. Courts apply them because they are law.

3. Certainty of law :

Statute law is so certain that parties apply them in their day -today

transactions, and, hence a great number of disputes do not go to courts.

3. Wider perspective:

According to the Realist, we may know the law by referring to case-law. But this is not enough. We must consult the Statues, Rules, Regulations etc. to know the law.

These criticisms apart, this-theory has its own advantages; It shows the reality behind the Statues, Rules and Regulations etc. through the medium of the Courts. This theory has gained a major victory in the United States.

Ch. 12-4 Law as a system of Rules - HART'S theory .

Hart's theory concerns itself with the analysis of the term "rule" or with a system of rules.

i. These rules deal with what "ought to be done". They are imperative and prescriptive. They have some characters of "commands". They demand repeated activity. Sometimes they are consti- tutive, e.g. rules of grammar. In others, regulative, as in rules of games like tennis, football etc.

These rules are followed as part of the game. Hence, observance of law by the people is part of an ordered tolerable society.

ii. The rules have two aspects:

a. external behavior and

b. Internal attitude that a behavior is obligatory.

Hart explains that when a person conducts himself to a certain pattern, he requires the same in others; if others do not confirm, he criticises them. To a rule or a set of rules, this is the reaction in the society.

iii. People comply or follow the rules not under coercion, but out of a sense of obligation. Even those who are opposed, consider the rule as an obligation to obey. Hence, law is followed under obligation and, not under coercion or force.
iv. There are the moral and legal rules in the society; moral rules apply to every human act, but, legal rule (law) applies to a number of such actions. These moral or legal rules apply to individuals whether they like them or not. They are non-optional.
v. Out of these legal rules has grown a system called the "legal system". Hart's view is that this system has arisen from the combination of the primary and secondary rules.

Primary rules are those which impose duties. Secondary rules

are those which confer the power of rule-making in the legal system and vests it in an authority eg. Parliament or any other authority. This makes uniform, dynamic rules adapting the social changes..

Criticism:

Though Hart's theory of law is convincing and has its own merits, still it has many draw-backs.

i. The division of rules into primary and secondary is not satisfactory. Change in the legislative sovereign may create problems.
ii. It is not correct to say that the entire legal system is based on rules. There are many fundamental principles which are

exclusive and separate, and are found in every developed legal system.

iii.   Observance of rules on the basis of internal or external atti- tudes expecting others to follow them, is not true in reality.

iv.   Hart's analysis of Rule is incomplete in respect of his expla- nation of "**What ought to be done**". The truth is, that people have found the necessity of a social life. In that a legal system is a must, and, basic rules are essential in such a system.

THE END

PART-2

Introductory

Jurisprudence is the study of law which penetrates to the theory and philosophy of law as a discipline. The term *'Juris'* denotes law and *'Prudence'* stands for knowledge, but this knowledge of law is not limited to study of statute books and case pronouncements only but spreads to the extensive knowledge of origin, development and scope of law and the concept of justice. Since this brief hand out is only indicative of the content of the curriculum, students are advised to familiarize themselves with all the recommended readings and participate in discussions in the class.

Chapter-1-Major Legal Systems of the World Today

(Abstract based on the writings of Rene David & John E.C. Brierley)

The major three types of legal systems of the world today are the Romano- Germanic family, the Common law family and the family of Socialist law. There are other systems also, situated outside these three traditions or sharing only part of their concepts.

Romano-Germanic family

A first family may be called the Romano-Germanic family. Here the rules of law are conceived as rules of conduct intimately linked to ideas of justice and morality. A major feature of this family is that the law has evolved, primarily for historical reasons, as an essentially private law, as a means of regulating the private relationships between individual citizens. The Romano-Germanic family of laws originated in Europe with the compilations of the Emperor Justinian (A.D. 483-565), evolved and developed a juridical science common to all and adapted to the conditions of the modern world. Through colonization by European nations, the Romano-Germanic family has conquered vast territories where the legal systems either belong or are related to this family. The phenomenon of voluntary "reception" has produced the same result in other countries which were not colonized.

In many of the countries outside Europe it has been possible to "receive" European laws, even though they possessed their own civilization. In the case of some Muslim countries the reception of European law and the adhesion to the Romano-Germanic family have been only partial, leaving some legal relations subject to the principles of the traditional, local law. In the countries of Africa and America, with their geographical

conditions and populations' distribution, creating conditions entirely different from those in Europe, have not led to the development of laws substantially different from their European models.

Common law family

A second family is that of the Common law, including the law of England and those laws modeled on English law. The Common Law, altogether different in its characteristics from the Romano-Germanic family, was formed primarily by judges who had to resolve specific disputes. The origins of the Common law are linked to royal power. It was developed as a system in those cases where the peace of the English kingdom was threatened, or when some other important consideration required, or justified, the intervention of royal power. The divisions of the Common law, its concepts and vocabulary, and the methods of the Common law lawyer, are entirely different from those of the Romano-Germanic family.

In certain extra-European countries, the Common law may have been only partially received as in the case, for example, of certain of Muslim countries or India and where it was received, attention was given to its transformation or adoption by reason of its co-existence with the tradition of previous civilizations. This observation is particularly true with respect of the Common law family because it groups some countries such as the United States and Canada where a civilization different in many respects from that of England has developed. The laws of these countries enjoy a largely autonomous place within the family.

Relations between these two families

Over the centuries there have been numerous contacts between countries of the Romano-Germanic family and those of the Common law, and the two families have tended, particularly in recent years, to draw closer together. In both, the law has under gone the influence of Christian morality and, since the Renaissance, philosophical teachings have given prominence to individualism, liberalism and personal rights. The laws of Scotland, Israel, the Union of South Africa and the Province of Quebec and in which the place and function of law are very different from what they are in the West. A true picture of law in contemporary world society would be incomplete without taking these considerations into account.

Family of Socialist Laws

The Socialist legal system makes up a third family, distinct from the first two. To date the members of the socialist camp are those countries which formerly belonged to the Romano-Germanic family, and they have preserved some of the characteristics of Romano-Germanic law. The originality of Socialist law is particularly evident because of its revolutionary nature; in opposition to the somewhat static character of Romano- Germanic laws, the proclaimed ambition of socialist jurists is to overturn society and create the conditions of a new social order in which the very concepts of state and law will disappear. However, legal science as such is not principally counted upon to create the new order: law according to Marxism-Leninism- a scientific truth-is strictly subordinate to the task of creating a new economic structure. In execution of this teaching, all means of production have been collectivized. As a result, private law has lost its pre-eminence — all law has now become public law.

The family of Socialist laws originated in the Union of Soviet Socialist Republics where these ideas prevailed and a new law has developed since the 1917 Revolution. However, the laws of the socialist or people's republics of Europe and Asia must be classed as groups distinct from Soviet law. These laws belong to the Socialist family.

The Far East Legal Systems

Far Eastern countries reject this view. For the Chinese, law is an instrument of arbitrary action rather than the symbol of Justice; it is a factor contributing to social disorder rather than to social order. The good citizen must not concern himself with law; he should live in a way which excludes thoughts of his rights or any recourse to the justice of courts. The Chinese communist regime and the westernization of Japan have not fundamentally changed this conception rooted as it in their ancient civilizations. Codes on the European model have been instituted in Japan but the people make little use of them; people abstain from using the courts and the courts themselves encourage litigants to resort to reconciliation; and new techniques have been developed for applying or removing the need of applying the law.

Muslim, Hindu, and Jewish Laws

In Muslim countries, more attention is given to the model law linked to the Islamic religion than to local custom or the laws and decrees of the sovereign and neither of these is thought to possess the full dignity of law. The same can be said of Jewish law and, in a very different context, Hindu law. Muslim and Hindu law, therefore, must be included within the major contemporary legal systems. Jewish law, despite its historical and philosophical interest, must be omitted because its sphere of influence is incomparably less than that the other two. In the Islamic and Hindu communities, law is held to be a necessary part of, indeed a basis for, society.

Black Africa and Malagasy Republic

The preceding observations regarding the Far East apply as well to the black African countries and the Malagasy Republic (Madagascar). Even though, Western laws adopted in Africa are often hardly, the vast majority of the population still lives according to traditional ways which do not comprise what the West calls law but rating it as nothing more than an artificially implanted body of rules.

* * * * * *

Our Legal System

(Abstract based on the article of Prof.N.R. Madhava Menon)

The legal system of a country is part of its social system and reflects the social, political, economic and cultural characteristics of that society. It is, therefore, difficult to understand the legal system outside the socio-cultural milieu in which it operates. It is true in the case of India also even though the legal system we now have is largely the gift of the British rulers.

Components of a Legal System

A legal system consists of certain basic principles and values (largely outlined by the Constitution), a set of operational norms including rights and duties of citizens spelt out in the laws -Central, State and local, institutional structures for enforcement of the laws and a cadre of legal personnel endowed with the responsibility of administering the system.

The Constitution: The Fundamental Law of the Land

India is declared to be a Socialist, Secular, Democratic Republic. It is said to have a quasi-federal structure. The Constitution of India represents the collective will of more than one billion Indians and, as such, the reservoir of enormous power. The form of government in India is democratic and republican and the method is parliamentary through adult franchise.

- The main goals are spelt out in Preamble itself which seeks to secure to all citizens:

"Justice, social, economic and political; Liberty of thought, expression, faith and worship; Equality of status and of opportunity, and to promote among them all." Fraternity assuring dignity of the individual and the "unity and integrity of Nation".

- Towards achieving the goals set out in the Preamble, the Constitution guarantees certain fundamental rights along with a machinery to enforce those rights to the people
- Further, towards achieving the goals set out in the Preamble, the Constitution gives certain Directives to State to follow in its policies and programmes.
- The Constitution envisages a unique place for the judiciary. This offers a cheap and expeditious remedy to the citizen to enforce the guaranteed rights.
- The Rule of Law is supreme and the independence of judiciary is reality in our country.

Laws, Civil and Criminal

The laws of the country are too numerous, varied and complex, inspired by the Constitution, Parliament, State legislatures and local councils make and unmake the laws day in and day out as the occasion demands. Courts interpret them in specific fact situations and, in the process, extend the scope and application of the laws. On the basis of the remedies sought and the procedure followed, all laws can be grouped into two categories, namely, Civil Laws and Criminal Laws. Broadly speaking, criminal law is concerned with wrongs against the community as a whole, while civil law is related to the rights duties and obligations of individual members of the community between themselves.

Civil Laws

Civil law includes a number of aspects which may be grouped under six or seven major headings such as family law, the law of property, the law of tort, the law of contract, the law relating to commerce and business, labour law, law of taxation etc. Family law, governs marriage, divorce, maintenance, custody of children, adoption inheritance and succession. The law of property includes rights of ownership, transfer, mortgages, trusts, intestacy and similar matters. The law of contracts, is concerned with the enforcement of obligations arising from agreements and promises. Injuries to person or property caused by failure to take reasonable care and caution leads to actionable wrongs under tort, which usually compensates the victim of such injuries. Laws of commerce and business, which includes contract law, relate to economic operations of

individuals, partnerships and companies and governmental regulation of them. Even law

of taxation forms part of commercial laws. Labour law deals with the relationship between employer and employees in the production and distribution of wealth.

Criminal law

Criminal Law is concerned with public wrongs or wrongs against the order and well being of the society in general. The persons guilty of such wrongs are prosecuted and punished by the State. These wrongs are specific and are defined in the Penal Code and a few other special and local laws. One important aspect in this regard is that criminal laws insist (apart from a few exceptional offences) on a particular intent or state of mind as a necessary ingredient of a criminal offence. Ignorance of law is never taken as an excuse.

Procedural Laws, Civil and Criminal

The Civil and Criminal Procedure Codes and the Evidence Act apply to judicial proceedings in the courts. The writ procedure under Articles 32 and 226 is unique to the Supreme Court and High Courts and is intended for the quick enforcement of Fundamental Rights whenever they are threatened by the State or its agencies.

For the enforcement of civil rights and obligations a suit before a civil court is usually instituted. The procedures for trial and appeals including execution of decrees and orders are laid down in the Code of Civil Procedure. The Limitation Act prescribes the

periods of limitation with in which suits can be filed. The Evidence Act regulates the relevancy, admissibility and probative value of evidence led in courts, civil and criminal.

Pleading and Civil Actions

A civil procedure commences with 'pleadings', which set out the precise question in dispute or the cause of action. The opposite party (the defendant) may file a written statement to admit or deny the allegations in the plaint. A party can appear himself in court for the hearing or make appearance through an agent or a pleader. According to the Advocates Act right to practice law before courts is given to Advocates only. The trial involves recording of evidence of witnesses on a day-to-day basis at the conclusion of which judgment is to be pronounced in open court. Because civil proceedings are private matters, they can at any time be abandoned or compromised and, in fact, in a number of cases they are settled before trial. Judgments are enforceable through the authority of the court.

Trial and Criminal proceedings

Criminal proceedings are designed to give every accused a 'fair trial' consistent with the constitutional commitment to individual liberty and freedom. A criminal proceeding

involves four major stages, namely, investigation, prosecution, trial and disposition.

Crimes being wrongs against society, the State undertakes the prosecution on behalf of the victim. The police on receiving information of the commission of an offence proceeds with the investigation. The arrested person has right to seek the aid of a lawyer of his choice and he cannot be compelled to give evidence against himself. Under our law every accused is presumed innocent and the prosecution (the State) has to prove the guilt beyond a reasonable doubt. If there is any doubt in the evidence or the prosecution, the benefit of doubt is given to the accused and he is acquitted. If at the end of trial, the Judge finds him guilty, he has a right to be heard on the determination of sentence.

Alternative Dispute Resolution System

Apart from the civil and criminal proceedings prescribed in the respective codes, there are a variety of adjudicative procedures followed in tribunals, quasi judicial administrative agencies, arbitration councils, nyaya panchayats etc. where private disputes are processed and settled through informal procedures. They are found to be cheap, expeditious and less cumbersome in terms of adjudication. Legal Aid clauses in laws provide poor persons with the services of lawyers to appear on their behalf.

Courts of Law

The Constitution itself provides for the Supreme Court and the High Court in each State at the apex of the judicial system and confers original and appellate jurisdiction on them primarily to resolve disputes between Union and the State, State and State, State and the citizen and in limited cases appeals arising out of private disputes involving substantial questions of law. Citizens can directly approach the High Courts or the Supreme Court to seek redress for the violation of Fundamental Rights. The High Courts and Supreme Court enjoy civil and criminal jurisdiction apart from the writ jurisdiction.

The State judiciary under the High Court is organized in a hierarchy on the civil and criminal sides based on their jurisdiction, territorial or monetary. On the criminal side, the Criminal Procedure Code provides for the Magistrates Court (First or second Class depending on the extent of powers for punishment) and above them the Sessions Courts, usually one in each District. On the civil side the Civil Procedure Code provides for the Munsiffs' Court (with limited pecuniary jurisdiction), the Sub-Divisional Court and the District Court each with varying pecuniary and territorial jurisdiction. There can be Special Courts set up for specific purposes and also Administrative and Revenue Tribunals to adjudicate upon specific categories of disputes. Appeals from these courts

and tribunals usually lie to the High Courts and, in exceptional cases, a second appeal

to the Supreme Court.

Judges

All judicial officers are free to administer law without fear or favour and they cannot be interfered with by anyone including the top functionary of the Government. The President, acting on the advice of the Cabinet and the Chief Justice of India, appoints the Judges of the Supreme Court and the High Court. The Governor of the State appoints the Judicial Officers of the State similarly on the advice of the State High Court/Government.

Lawyers and the Bar

Lawyers are officers of court and are constituted into an independent profession under the Advocates Act,1961. Without the expert assistance of lawyers on either side of a dispute, judges will find it difficult to find the truth on disputed facts in issue and interpret the law applicable to varied situations. That is why the legal profession is often referred to as a noble and a learned profession. Legal Services to the poor is one of the social obligation of every lawyer required under the Bar Council rules of professional conduct.

* * * * *

The Indian Legal System

(Abstract based on the Article of Joseph Minattur)

A Historical Account of the Indian Legal System

Three main streams join together to form the Indian legal system. That of the common law is perhaps the most dominant among them. Then there is the stream of laws springing from religion. The third is that of the civil ('Romanist') law which energizes the system with unruffled ethical verve and accords comeliness to its contours. Trickles of customary laws cherished by tribal societies and other ethnic communities also flow into the main stream. In the year 1788, a codification of Hindu law on contracts and succession was proposed by Sir William Jones to Lord Cornwallis. On 18 May 1783 "A Regulation for forming into a Regular Code, was passed by the Governor-General and Council. Speaking on the Charter Bill of 1833 Macaulay said:

"I believe that no country ever stood so much in need of a code of laws as India, and I believe also that never was a country in which they want might so easily be supplied."

- The first Law Commission immediately after its appointment in 1833 with Macaulay as its President took up the task of codification. Under Macaulay's personal direction it prepared its first draft of the Indian Penal Code and submitted it to the Governor-General in Council on 14 October 1837.
- The second Law Commission which sat in London from 1853 to 1856 emphasized that such a body of law ought to be prepared with a constant regard to the conditions and institutions of India, and the character, religious and usages of the population.
- The Commission gave final shape to Macaulay's Penal Code and the Legislative Council adopted the Code of Civil Procedure in 1859, the Penal Code in 1860 and the Code of Criminal Procedure in 1861.
- The third law Commission, appointed in 1861, was enjoined to prepare for India a body of substantive law, in preparing which the law of England should be used as a basis.
- The fourth law Commission expressed a similar view when it recommended in 1879 that English law should be made the basis in a great measure of our future Codes.
- It is generally assumed that India is a common law country. Indian codes or judicial procedure owe a great deal to procedure in England. But with the introduction of nyaya panchayats (village tribunals) which are indigenous in origin the English procedure has been virtually replaced at the grass root level.

- With the reign of dharma which may be equated with equity while it comprises the concept of law unopposed to justice, there was no need in India to think of a separate branch of law known as equity detached from common law.
- In the early nineteen sixties a number of territories where the civil law prevailed became parts of the Indian Union. In the Union territory of Goa, Daman and Diu, Portuguese civil law was in force, even after the extension of several Indian enactments to the territory, it is generally the provisions of the Portuguese Civil Code which apply to the people of this territory in matters of personal law.
- In the former French settlements of Pondicherry. Karaikal, Mahe and Yanam which, when ceded, were formed into the Union territory now known as Pondicherry, there are Indian citizens who are governed in matters of personal law by the provisions of the French civil code as they existed at the time of the cession.
- The customary laws of various tribal communities and other ethnic groups also form part of the law administered in India. To cite one instance: matriliny among the Mappila Muslims of Kerala, though not favored by the tenets of Islam, is permitted to play a decisive role in the rules of succession applicable to them.

In the light of the presence laws based on religion of the several communities, it would be more justified to regard the Indian Legal System as a mixed system. The mosaic of Indian law may have a large number of common law pieces; but marble quarried from France and Portugal, gold leaves brought from Arabia and clusters of Precious stones gleaned from Indian fields do deserve to be discarded. When India adopts a civil code, under the directive in the Constitution it is likely to be eclectic in character, it may have in it a harmonious admixture of various laws based on religion and customary laws, as well as provisions derived from western codes and the English common law. What the Napoleonic code has done for continental Europe, the Americas, and parts of Asia and Africa, a well-framed Indian civil code may easily do for south and Southeast Asia.

* * * * *

Introduction to the Legal Process

This chapter focuses on the scheme and methods of the study of law as a discipline. The essay is based on comments made orally to a Faculty Colloquium of the Faculty of Law, and visiting professors to the University of Delhi in January and February, 1969.

The Object of Law Study

- In one sense, "law" is a large body of rules and regulations, based mainly on general principles of justice, fair play and convenience, have been worked out by governmental bodies to regulate human activities and define what is and what is not permissible conduct in various situations.
- Such rules and regulations are sometimes found in our state and federal constitutions, more often in statutes, sometimes in administrative rulings, and in many instances have been developed by the courts themselves in the process of deciding the controversies that come before them.
- To illustrate, when there is evidence that some person has killed another, or has robbed or stolen or done some other act disruptive of the public peace of welfare, not only do we assert that he has "broken the law" but we expect that the appropriate agencies of government will in accordance with the rules of law, apprehend and bring him before the proper court, conduct a fair and orderly trial to determine his guilt or innocence, and if he is guilty, prescribe and carry out appropriate corrective or punitive measures.
- This whole legal process is carried on through the various organs of government by a large number of people - legislators, lawyers, judges, police officers, administrative officials, and many others, most of whom must be intensively trained in various aspects of the system.
- Law schools are engaged primarily in training future lawyers, judges and others who will operate this legal system. Thus the study of law necessarily involves not only a study of legal rules but also a study of the whole legal system through which society attempts to maintain "law and order".
- Students are learning rules of law and studying the court decisions and legal proceedings in which they are applied, to enable you to solve legal problems as they are solved by our legal system.
- If, on the other hand, you know a lot of legal rules but can't apply them and work out a reasonably accurate solution of the everyday legal problems you run into, you simply haven't learned what a lawyer has to know.
- Whenever you are reading a law book or discussing a problem in class or reviewing, keep this one thing in mind you're not merely memorizing what the courts and legislatures have said and done in the past.

- You're trying to learn how the legal system works and how to solve future legal problems in accordance with the principles that have been established.

Studying Law under the "Case Method" or "Case System"

- The "Case system" is based on the idea that the best way to study law is to study the actual court decisions in various types of cases and to derive from them, by inductive reasoning, an understanding of the main fields or classifications in the law and the general rules and principles of law applicable in those fields.
- If you are studying law under this system you should know the best methods of doing these.

"Cases" and "Case Books"

- Before you can properly read and "brief" the cases in your casebook, it is essential that you understand what they are, how they came to be written, where the author of your case book got them, and what is in them.
- Cases, as we shall use the term in this discussion, are the published reports of controversies which have come before the courts, including the court's decision and its reasons for the decision.
- Once the majority of judges have approved an opinion, it is "handed over" together with any dissenting opinions. Then, it is given out to the parties and made public in the one way or another.
- After they are published, these opinions of "cases" are customarily referred to or "cited" by giving the name of the case, the volume number, name and page of the state report in which it is published.
- A case you read in your case book is normally, an exact copy of what some judge has written in explanation of his court's decision in a particular law suit brought to that court for decision.

Reading Cases

- The fundamental thing in reading cases is to know what to look for. Otherwise you may concentrate on the wrong thing or miss an important point.
- The first thing you will usually find in a case is a brief statement of the kind of controversy involved. That is, whether it was criminal prosecution, an action of tort for damages, an action for breach of contract, or to recover land, etc.
- The next thing you will usually find is a statement of the facts of the controversy, who the parties were, what they did, what happened to them, who brought the action and what he wanted.

- Next comes a statement of the question or questions the court is called upon to decide the various "issues" (either of law or fact) which must be settled before a decision on the controversy can be reached. Any of you who have done any debating, understand "issues", the breaking up of a general problem into specific sub-problems.
- After the issues comes the arguments, on them a discussion of the pros and cons. This is where logic comes into play. You will recall that there are two main types of logical reasoning -inductive and deductive. Inductive reasoning involves the formulation of general propositions from a consideration of specific problems or observations; deductive reasoning involves the application of a general proposition already formulated to some specific situation or problem so that a conclusion can be drawn as to it.
- If there happens to be a statute or constitutional provision prescribing a general rule as to questions like those involved in the case, the judge has his major premise and will devote his argument to a consideration of its scope and applicability to the issues in the case.
- If there is no statute or other prescribed general rule, the judge will try by induction to derive one from the decisions and opinions to previous cases involving issues similar to those in the present case, or from general principles of fairness, policy and common sense, and then apply it to the issues at hand and deduce his conclusion.
- Finally, after the argument on all the issues the judge states the general conclusion to be drawn there from, and winds up the opinion with a statement of the Court's decision.
- On reading the case, first get a clear picture of the controversy involved. Get all the facts and issues straight. Consider the following:

a. What kind of an action it is,

b. Who the parties were,

c. What they did and what happened to them,

d. Who brought the action, what he wanted,

e. What the defence was,

f. What happened in the lower court (if it's a case of appeal),

g. How the case got to this court,

h. Just what this court had to decide.

- At this point, stop for a moment. Look at the problem first from the plaintiff's point of view, then from the defendant's. Ask yourself how you would decide it, what you think the decision ought to be. Now read the argument and the court's conclusions
  - In thus analyzing the court's argument and conclusions it is important to distinguish carefully between the rules and propositions of law actually relied upon by the court in deciding the issues involved in the case (these are called "holdings")
- Other legal propositions and discussion which you may find in the opinion but which are not relevant nor applicable to the issues before the court (these are called "dicta"). Dicta, not being relevant to the issues before the court, was probably not argued by counsel nor thoroughly considered by the court.
- Courts in each jurisdiction regard their own prior "holdings" as creating binding precedents which they feel obliged to follow in later cases involving the same issues. This is called the doctrine of stare decisis and makes for stability and predictability in the law.

The Case Method from the Students' Point of View

One of the important developments of Indian Legal Education in the last few years is the introduction of the "case method" of teaching in several Indian Law Faculties. The "case method" sometimes called the "discussion method" is a term that has been used to describe a wide variety of teaching methods, but the one common element of these methods usually is the use of actual court opinions as the basis of analysis and discussion in the law classes.

- The sine qua non of good classes using the case method is prepared by students who have had access to cases prior to class, and who have and analyzed those cases.
- When the case method is used as a teaching technique, examinations usually take the form of hypothetical fact situations, i.e. a hypothetical case, calling upon the student to decide the case and give his reasons, or calling upon the student to play the advocate's role and write the best possible arguments for one side or another of the case.
  - An ideal case study method can be divided into the following five parts:

1. **Study before class**: Students' practice in the case method is often to use a key or guide for analyzing law cases. The key or guide has four parts: the facts, the essential question, the answer or court decision on that question, and the

reasons for that decision. Each law case can be analyzed into these four parts, and such analysis is often called a "case brief".

F: (Facts: a brief two or three line summary of the essential facts of the case i.e. those facts necessary for the decision.)

Q: (Question: a one line question formed to pose the major issue in the case).

D: (Decision: The court's holding: Something this can be "Yes" or "no" in answer to the question. The court's order can then be stated, e.g. "affirmed", "appeal dismissed", etc.)

R: (Reasons: Here the reasons can be listed in number outline form).

2. The Classroom Discussion: In class, the student should have his brief in front of him. The teacher may call on a particular student to begin the discussion by stating the case, i.e. by stating in turn the facts, question, decision, and reasons, from his case brief. The student should try to take brief notes during class to jot down the important points brought out in class.
3. Study or Review after Class: It is always useful, if there is time, to review the subjects which were discussed in class immediately after that class, to add to one's notes, and to clear up any questions one has in his mind. This is a key step

in his thinking and learning, and one vitally different from the lecture method. If

this outlining is short circuited, then the student misses the understanding and he will be unable to cope with a well constructed examination which should attempt to test his understanding and not just his memory.

4. Preparing for the Examination: At the end of the term, the student should complete his outlining for any portions of the course for which he has not completed it before. One effective technique of studying at this stage, which many students use, is a small discussion group, usually of three students in the same course.
5. Writing the Examination: Here a few simple guidelines may help. First, allocate your time wisely. Second, outline your answer before you begin to write. Particularly with the problem or hypothetical type examination question, it is important to spend about one third of your allocated time in analyzing and thinking through the problem. Jot down on a spare piece of paper a rough outline of your answer, and only then begin to write. Third, write legibly.

- The important thing to remember, is that the purpose of the whole process- studying, classroom discussion, examinations, etc. is to give you a basic understanding of the law, its sources, its rules and their limitations and the reasons for those rules. It is not enough to simply ascertain "what is the law", in some general abstract sense. There are other relevant questions which can be posed also, such as "What should be the law".

- First might be called the "planning transacting" approach. In a given situation, a lawyer may be called upon to advise a client about the best way to go about some business or personal activity. At this stage the prime consideration is getting the objectives accomplished with the least risk of something going wrong.
- Second might be called the "predicting" approach. In some circumstances the lawyer is called upon to perform a task which basically is to predict how a court might rule on a question. Justice Holmes, in the U.S. is quoted as saying that law is nothing more nor less than a prediction of what the courts will do in a particular circumstance.
- Third might be called the "advocacy" approach. For instance a client has decided to bring a law suit (either with or against his lawyer's advice). Now it is the lawyer's task to do the best job of advocacy which he can do for his client. In this approach it is his task to marshal the strongest arguments, not to predict, nor to "avoid" problem issues.
- Fourth, and finally, comes the "judicial" or "legislative" approach. In this instance the lawyer (as a judge, legislator, member of a

commission or committee, etc.) is called upon to give his view as to what the law should be

Each of those tasks or approaches requires skills a bit different from the other. It is important for the law student to develop his talents in each of these directions. One way of doing this is to occasionally analyze a case, either in his private studies or in classroom discussion, according to each of these approaches.

* * * * *

Learning the Law

(Abstract based on the writings of Glanville Williams)

Case Law Technique- *Ratio Decidendi* and *Obiter Dictum*

English courts make a habit of following their previous decisions within more or less well-defined limits. This is called the doctrine of precedent. The part of a case that is said to possess authority is the ratio decidendi, that is to say, the rule of law upon which the decision is founded.

- What the doctrine of precedent declares is that cases must be decided the same way when their material facts are the same. The legally material facts may recur in future cases and it is with these that the doctrine is concerned.
- The ratio decidendi of a case can be defined as the material facts of the case plus the decision thereon. Suppose that in a certain case facts A, B and C exist; and suppose that the court finds that facts B and C are material and fact A immaterial, and then reaches conclusion X (e.g. judgment for the plaintiff, or judgment for the defendant). Then the doctrine of precedent enables us to say that in any future case in which facts B and C exist, or in which facts A and B

and C exist, the conclusion must be X. If in a future case facts A, B, C and D

exist, the fact D is held to be material, the first case will not be a direct authority, though it may be of value as an analogy.

- Material nature of facts depends on the particular case, but take as an illustration a "running down" action, that is to say, an action for injuries sustained through the defendant's negligent driving of a vehicle. The fact that the plaintiff had red hair and freckles, that his name was Smith, and that the accident happened on a Friday are immaterial, for the rule of law upon which the decision proceeds will apply equally to persons who do not possess these characteristics and to accidents that happen on other days. On the other hand, the fact that the defendant drove negligently, and the fact that in consequence he injured the plaintiff, are material, and a decision in the plaintiff's favour on such facts will be an authority for the proposition that a person is liable for causing damage through the negligent driving of a vehicle.
- The foregoing is a general explanation of the phrase "the ratio decidendi of a case." To get a clearer idea of the way in which a ratio decidendi is extracted, let us take a decided case and study it in detail. The case of Wilkinson v. Downton [1897] 2 QB 57, where the plaintiff was awarded damages by a jury for nervous shock, and the trial judge then heard argument on the question whether the verdict could be upheld in law. The first part of the judgment, which is all that needs be considered here, runs as follows.

WRIGHT, J. – In this case the defendant, represented to the plaintiff that her husband was smashed up in an accident, and was lying at The Elms at Leytonstone with both legs broken, and that she was to go at once in a cab with two pillows to fetch him home. All this was false. The effect of the statement of the plaintiff was a violent shock to her nervous system, producing vomiting and other serious and permanent physical consequences as well as expense to her husband for medical attendance. The statement was a misrepresentation intended to be acted on to the damage of the plaintiff. The real question is as to the

£100, the greatest part of which is given as compensation for the female plaintiff's illness and suffering. The defendant has, as I assume for the moment, willfully done an act calculated to cause physical harm to the plaintiff – that is to say, to infringe her legal right to personal safety, and has in fact thereby caused physical harm to her. It would be a grave approach to a civilized system of law if it did not give a remedy on such facts.

- Let us now see how the ratio decidendi is to be extracted. This is done by finding the material facts. The defendant by way of what was meant to be a

joke told the plaintiff that the latter's husband had been smashed up in an

accident. The plaintiff, who had previously been of normal health, suffered a shock and serious illness. Wright, J. held that the defendant was liable, not perhaps for the tort of deceit but because the defendant had willfully done an act calculated to cause physical harm to the plaintiff, and had in fact caused such harm.

- To find the ratio decidendi, one may notice the detailed facts as may be deemed to be material, plus the decision on the facts. This would result in the following rule: that where the defendant has willfully told the plaintiff a lie of a character that is likely (a clearer word that "calculated") to frighten and so cause physical harm to the plaintiff, and it has in fact caused such harm, the defendant is liable, in the absence of some ground justification.
- The defendant did not confine his judgment to lies, but spoke only of wilfully doing an act which is calculated to and does cause physical harm; and this gives us the true ratio. It was immaterial that the particular form of mischief perpetrated by the defendant took the form of a verbal lie; it might have been some other act likely to cause harm, and the legal outcome would have been the same.
- What is really involved in finding the ratio decidendi of a case is a process of abstraction. Abstraction is the mental operation of picking out certain qualities and relations from the facts of experience. Imagine a baby in whose household

there is a terrier called Caesar. The baby will be taught to call this dog "bow- wow," because, "bow-wow" is easier to say than "Caesar." The individual dog Caesar is, at a low level of abstraction, a terrier; at a higher level he is a dog; higher still, a mammal and then an animal and a living thing.

- The ascertainment of the ratio decidendi of a case depends upon a process of abstraction from the totality of facts that occurred in it. The higher the abstraction, the wider the ratio decidendi. Thus "telling a lie" or "doing any act with intent to affect the plaintiff in body or mind" is a wrongful act could be the ratio decidendi of this case in a wider sense.
- We carry on the process of abstraction until all the particular facts have been eliminated except the fact of the doing of an act that is intended to affect the plaintiff adversely and is likely to cause physical harm; and the fact of the occurrence of such harm to find the ratio decidendi.
- The ratio decidendi could be found primarily by reading what the judge says in his judgment, but partly also our knowledge of the law in general, and by our common sense and our feeling for what the law ought to be. The finding of the ratio decidendi is not an automatic process; it calls for lawyerly skill and knowledge.
- The rule stated by Wright, J. refers to a person who has "willfully" done an act calculated to cause physical harm, and the primary meaning of a "willful" act is one that is done with the intention of bringing about a particular consequence.

Downton did not, perhaps, intend to cause Mrs. Wilkinson a serious illness, but he did intend to frighten her, and that was sufficient, the word "willful" is, indeed, capable of extending to recklessness. In analysis, the case is one of recklessness as to the plaintiff's fright, not one of intention as to the fright; but the legal liability should be, and is, the same.

- One may argue that there is another unnecessary limitation contained in the judgment is that the judge referred to the fact that the plaintiff had been in normal health, yet it is not possible but probable that the decision would have been just the same even if her health had previously been poor. However, on a mature consideration and when the question arises, it could be decided that this limitation is unnecessary.
- As regards precedents, often judges may be gravely dissatisfied with a given case and yet, owing to the excessively strict doctrine of precedent, it may be impossible for them to overrule it. In such circumstances it is simply human nature that they will distinguish it if they can. The limit of the process is reached when a judge says that the precedent is an authority only "on its actual facts." For most practical purposes this is equivalent to announcing that it will never be followed.

Obiter Dicta

In contrast with the ratio decidendi is the obiter dictum. The latter is a mere saying by the way, a chance remark, which is not binding upon future courts, though it may be respected according to the reputation of the judge, the eminence of the court, and the circumstances in which it came to be pronounced. An example would be a rule of law stated merely by way of analogy or illustration, or a suggested rule upon which the decision is not finally rested.

- The reason for not regarding an obiter dictum as binding is that it was probably made without a full consideration of the cases on the point, and that, if very broad in its terms, it was probably made without a full consideration of all the consequences that may follow from it; or the judge may not have expressed a concluded opinion.
- When some observations are made in a case in which the point was not finally decided, and in any case such observations are not made the ground of the decision, those observations made upon it are to be treated as obiter.
- It is frequently said that a ruling based upon hypothetical facts is obiter. This is often true. Thus if the judge says: "I decide for the defendant; but if the facts had been properly pleaded I should have found for the plaintiff," the latter part of the statement is obiter.

If a decision would otherwise be a binding authority, it does not lose that status merely because the point was not argued by counsel. This is so, at least, where the precedent case is that of the same court. Distinction between ratio decidendi and obiter dicta should be clearly made out for a successful lawyering.

* * * * *

The Province of Jurisprudence Determined (Abstract of John Austin's writings)

The matter of jurisprudence is positive law: law, simply and strictly so called: or law set by political superiors to political inferiors. This is an attempt to determine the province of jurisprudence, or to distinguish the matter of jurisprudence from those various related objects.

- A law, in the most general and comprehensive acceptation in which the term, in its literal meaning, is employed, may be said to be a rule laid down for the guidance of an intelligent being by an intelligent being having power over him. In the comprehensive sense above indicated, the term law embraces the following objects:- Law set by God to his human creatures, and laws set by men to men.

- The whole or a portion of the laws set by God to men is frequently styled the law of nature, or natural law, those laws or rules, as considered collectively or in a mass, to be named as the Divine law, or the law of God.
  - Laws set by men to men are of two leading or principal classes;

  a. Some are established by political superiors, sovereign and subject: by persons exercising supreme and subordinate government, in independent nations, or independent political societies.
  b. Some others are not established by political superiors, or are not established by political superiors, in that capacity or character but being rules set and enforced by mere opinion.

- The aggregate of human laws properly so called belonging to the second of the classes above mentioned like human behaviour to specific situations, fashion and passion etc.
- Every law or rule (taken with the largest signification which can be given to the term properly) is a command. Or, rather, laws or rules, properly so called, are a species of commands.
  - A command in the words of Austin is "if you express or intimate a wish that I

shall do or forbear from some act, and if you will visit me with an evil in case I

comply not with your wish, the expression or intimation of your wish is a command."

- If one cannot or will not harm the other in case the latter comply not with the former's wish, the expression of the former's wish is not a command, although he utters his wish in imperative phrase.
- A command, then, is a signification of desire. But a command is distinguished from other significations of desire by this peculiarity: that the party to whom it is directed is liable to evil from the other, in case he comply not with the desire.
- Command and duty are, therefore, correlative terms: the meaning denoted by each being implied or supposed by the other. Or wherever a duty lies, a command has been signified; and whenever a command is signified, a duty is imposed.
- The evil which will probably be incurred in case a command be disobeyed or (to use an equivalent expression) in case a duty be broken, is frequently called a sanction, or an enforcement of obedience.
- It appears, then, from what has been premised, that the ideas or notions comprehended by the term command are the following:

  1. A wish or desire conceived by a rational being, that another rational being shall do or forbear.

2. An evil to proceed from the former, and to be incurred by the latter, in case the latter comply not with the wish.

3. An expression or intimation of the wish by words or other signs.

2. It also appears from what has been premised, that command, duty, and sanction are inseparably connected terms: that each embraces the same ideas as the others, though each denotes those ideas in a peculiar order or series.

3. Commands are of two species. Some are laws or rules. The others have not acquired an appropriate name, but could be called occasional or particular commands.'

4. Now where it obliges generally to acts or forbearances of a class, a command is a law or rule. But where it obliges to a specific act or forbearance, or to acts or forbearances which it determines specifically or individually, a command is occasional or particular.

5. To illustrate, if the Parliament prohibited simply the exportation of corn, either for a given period or indefinitely, it would establish a law or rule: a kind or sort of acts being determined by the command, and acts of that kind or sort being generally forbidden. But an order issued by Parliament to meet an impending

scarcity, and stopping the exportation of corn then shipped and in port, would

not be a law or rule, though issued by the sovereign legislature.

- If made by a sovereign assembly deliberately, and with the forms of legislation, it would probably be called a law. If uttered by an absolute monarch, without deliberation or ceremony, it would scarcely be confounded with acts of legislation, and would be styled an arbitrary command.
  - According to **Blackstone**, a law and a particular command are distinguished in the following manner:– A law obliges generally the members of the given community, or a law obliges generally persons of a given class. A particular command obliges a single person, or persons whom it determines individually.
  - However, to **Austin**, commands which oblige generally the members of the given community, or commands which oblige generally persons of given classes, are not always laws or rules.
- As per Austin's illustration, in which the sovereign commands that all corn actually shipped for exportation be stopped and detained; the command is obligatory upon the whole community, but as it obliges them only to a set of acts individually assigned, it is not a law.
- And, secondly, a command which obliges exclusively persons individually determined, may amount, notwithstanding, to a law or a rule. For example, A father may set a rule to his child or children: a guardian, to his ward: a master, to his slave or servant.

  - It appears, from what has been premised, that a law, properly so called, may be defined in the following manner.

    a. A law is a command which obliges a person or persons.
    b. A law is a command which obliges a person or persons to a course of conduct.
    c. Laws and other commands are said to proceed from superiors, and to bind or oblige inferiors.

  - But, taken with the meaning wherein I here understand it, the term superiority signifies might: the power of affecting others with evil or pain, and of forcing them, through fear of that evil, to fashion their conduct to one's wishes.
- For example, God is, emphatically, the superior of Man. For his power of affecting us with pain, and of forcing us to comply with his will, is unbounded and resistless.
  - To a limited extent, the sovereign One or Number is the superior of the subject or citizen: the master, of the slave or servant: the father, of the child.
- In short, whoever can oblige another to comply with his wishes, is the superior of that other, so far as the ability reaches:

The party who is exposed to the impending evil, being, to that same extent, the inferior.

- Remotely and indirectly, indeed, permissive laws are often or always imperative. For the parties released from duties are restored to liberties or rights: and duties answering those rights are, therefore, created or revived.
- An imperfect law is a law which wants a sanction, and which, therefore, is not binding. A law declaring that certain acts are crimes, but annexing no punishment to the commission of acts of the class, is the simplest and most obvious example.
- Speaking of imperfect obligations, they commonly mean duties which are not legal: duties imposed by commands of God, or duties imposed by positive morality, as contradistinguished to duties imposed by positive law.
- An imperfect obligation, in the other meaning of the expression, is a religious or a moral obligation. The term imperfect does not denote that the law imposing the duty wants the appropriate sanction. It denotes that the law imposing the duty is not a law established by a political superior.
- There are no laws merely creating rights. There are laws which merely create duties: Every law, really conferring a right, imposes expressly or tacitly a relative duty, or a duty correlating with the right.

- Every law, really conferring a right, is, therefore, imperative: as imperative, as if its only purpose were the creation of a duty, or as if the relative duty, which it inevitably imposes, were merely absolute.
- However, customary laws must be excepted from the proposition 'that laws are a species of commands as they are not the creatures of the sovereign or state, although the sovereign or state may abolish them at pleasure.
- At its origin, a custom is a rule of conduct which the governed observes spontaneously, or not in pursuance of a law set by a political superior. The custom is transmuted into positive law, when it is adopted as such by the courts of justice, and when the judicial decisions fashioned upon it are enforced by the power of the state.
- But before it is adopted by the courts, and clothed with the legal sanction, a custom is merely a rule of positive morality: a rule generally observed by the citizens or subjects.
- In 1815 the allied armies occupied France; and so long as the allied armies occupied France, the commands of the allied sovereigns were obeyed by the French government, and, through the French government, by the French people generally. But since the commands and the obedience were comparatively rare and transient, they were not sufficient to constitute the relation of sovereignty and subjection between the allied sovereigns and the members of the invaded nation. In spite of those commands, and in spite of that obedience, the French government was sovereign or independent. Or in spite of those commands, and in spite of that obedience, the French government and its subjects were an independent political society whereof the allied sovereigns were not the sovereign portion.
- It appears from what has preceded, that, in order that a given society may form a society political, the bulk of its members must be in a habit of obedience to a certain and common superior. But, in order that the given society may form a society political and independent, that certain superior must not be habitually obedient to a determinate human superior.
- Let us suppose, for example, that a viceroy obeys habitually the author of his delegated powers. And, to render the example complete, let us suppose that the viceroy receives habitual obedience from the generality or bulk of the persons who inhabit his province. Now though he commands habitually within the limits of his province, and receives habitual obedience from the generality or bulk of its inhabitants, the viceroy is not sovereign within the limits of his province, nor are he and its inhabitants an independent political society.

- Society formed by the intercourse of independent political societies, is the province of international law, or of the law obtaining between nations. For (adopting a current expression) international law, or the law obtaining between nations, is conversant about the conduct of independent political societies considered as entire communities.
- A given independent society, whose number may be called inconsiderable, is commonly esteemed a natural, and not a political society, although the generality of its members be habitually obedient or submissive to a certain and common superior.
- Let us suppose, for example, that a single family of savages lives in absolute estrangement from every other community. And let us suppose that the father, the chief of this insulated family, receives habitual obedience from the mother and children. Here the imperative father and chief a monarch or sovereign, or the obedient mother and children subjects.
- For the purpose of attacking an external enemy, or for the purpose of repelling an attack made by an external enemy, the generality or bulk of its members, who are capable of bearing arms, submits to one leader, or to one body of leaders. But as soon as that exigency passes, this transient submission ceases; and the society reverts to the state which may be deemed its ordinary state.
- In order that an independent society may form a society political, it must not fall short of a number which may be called considerable. And the lowest possible number which will satisfy that vague condition cannot be fixed precisely.
- Distinguishing political from natural society, Mr. Bentham, in his Fragment on Government, thus defines the former: 'When a number of persons (whom we may style subjects) are supposed to be in the habit of paying obedience to a person, or an assemblage of persons, of a known and certain description (whom we may call governor or governors), such persons altogether (subjects and governors) are said to be in a state of political society.'
- According to the definition of independent political society which is stated or supposed by Hobbes in his excellent treatises on government, a society is not a society political and independent, unless it can maintain its independence, against attacks from without, by its own intrinsic or unaided strength.
- In his great treatise on international law, Grotius defines sovereignty — Now in order that an individual or body may be sovereign in a given society, two essentials must unite. The generality of the given society must render habitual obedience to that certain individual or body; whilst that individual or body must not be habitually obedient to a determinate human superior.

- Sovereign power (according to Grotius) is perfectly or completely independent of other human power; inasmuch that its acts cannot be annulled by any human will other than its own.
  - According to Von Martens of Gottingen (the writer on positive international law already referred to), "a sovereign government is a government which ought not to receive commands from any external or foreign government."
- But Austin attacks these vies with the practical argument that "Every government, let it be never so powerful, renders occasional obedience to commands of other governments. Every government defers frequently to those opinions and sentiments which are styled international law. And every government defers habitually to the opinions and sentiments of its own subjects."
- An independent political society is divisible into two portions: namely, the portion of its members which is sovereign or supreme, and the portion of its members which is merely subject. In most actual societies, the sovereign powers are engrossed by a single member of the whole, or are shared exclusively by a very few of its members: and even in the actual societies whose governments are esteemed popular, the sovereign number is a slender portion of the entire political community.
- An independent political society governed by itself, or governed by a sovereign body consisting of the whole community, is not impossible: but the existence of such societies is so extremely improbable.

Governments which may be styled aristocracies are not infrequently distinguished into the three following forms: namely, oligarchies, aristocracies and democracies. If the proportion of the sovereign number to the number of the entire community be deemed extremely small, the supreme government is styled an oligarchy. If the proportion be deemed small, but not extremely small, the supreme government is styled an aristocracy. If the proportion be deemed large, the supreme government is styled popular, or is styled a democracy. A government which one man shall deem an oligarchy, will appear to another a liberal aristocracy: whilst a government which one man shall deem an aristocracy, will appear to another a narrow oligarchy. A government which one man shall deem a democracy, will appear to another a government of a few: whilst a government which one man shall deem an aristocracy, will appear to another a government of many. The proportion, moreover, of the sovereign number to the number of the entire community, may stand, it is manifest, at any point in a long series of minute degrees.

* * * * *

Positivism : British Theories

The start of the nineteenth century might be taken as marking the beginning of the positivist movement (Law is a product of positive action). This way of legal thinking considered law as a product of deliberate actions of authorities thereby moving away from the concept of natural law (Law as one derived from the principles of nature).

- The term 'positivism' has many meanings, which were tabulated by Professor Hart as follows:

1. Laws are commands:- This meaning is associated with the two founders of British positivism, Bentham and his disciple Austin
2. The analysis of legal concepts is (a) worth pursuing, (b) distinct from sociological and historical inquiries, (c) distinct from critical evaluation.
3. Decisions can be deduced logically from predetermined rules without recourse to social aims, policy or morality.
4. Moral judgments cannot be established or defended by rational argument, evidence or proof.
5. The law as it is actually laid down.

- Positivism, thus has to be kept separate from the law that ought to be. Whatever meanings are ascribed to positivism, it is contrasted with natural law, which also has different meanings.
- Positivism flourishes in stable social conditions; Bentham was a tireless campaigner for reform, and both he and Austin insisted that prior to reform there has to be a thorough-going clarification of the law as it is.
- The 'is', which positivists are anxious to preserve inviolate, is largely composed of 'oughts'. So far most positivists would agree but they would add that only those 'oughts' acquire the character of 'law' which have filtered through certain accepted criteria of validity.
- It follows that positivists need not deny that judges make law; indeed, the majority admit it. They also acknowledge the influence of ethical considerations on judges and legislators, and that generally it is because a principle to be moral and just when a judge or legislator adopted it.
- The quality of law originates irrespective of morality, so that even if an unjust proposition were embodied in precedent or statute, it would be 'law' none the less because it would exhibit the formal stamp of validity.
- On the contrary, Natural lawyers would assert that a proposition is 'law' not merely because it satisfies some formal requirement, but by virtue of an additional minimum moral content.
- According to Naturalists, an immoral rule would not be 'law' however much it may satisfy formal requirements [As explained by Justice. Sajjad Ahmad in Jilani

v.   Government of Punjab Pak, LD (1972) SC 139, 261].

- It is also thought to follow from the positivist obsession with the 'is' that they distinguish between formal analysis on one hand, and historical and functional analysis on the other.
- The suggested division between 'analytical' and 'functional' study is unhappier still. This leads to a moral general objection. It is said that a law is what its maker thought it ought to be, whether it be moral or immoral.
- In a situation uncovered by authority, for instance, a judge will enunciate as law an appropriate rule, which will lead to the desired decision; but the point is that he states the rule to be what he feels it ought to be.
- As Sir Garfield Barwick CJ said 'the common law is what the court, so informed, decides that it should be."
- Hence it is not correct to say that the function of the court in general is to declare what the law is and not to decide what it ought to be.
- A lower court is bound to apply an undistinguishable precedent of a superior court, however, wrong it may be, so that, with regard to such court, there is a distinction between what 'is' and what 'ought to be law'.
- A superior court, however, when overruling the unjust precedent declares that it never was law notwithstanding the formal stamp of validity which it had borne until then. With regard to such a court the 'is'/'ought' separation in precedent as a criterion of identification breaks down at that point.
- Repeal of a statute, on the other hand, takes effect only from the date of repeal, and even when the effect of repeal is expressly made retroactive, there is no denial that the repealed statute was law until it was repealed.
- The introduction of morality into the criterion of identification of laws presents difficulties. Morality is a diffuse idea and no one, even a naturalists, maintains that everything which is moral is 'law'.
- Since the area of 'law' is bound to be narrower than that of morality, its boundary should be made as clear as possible. Thus, there is a difference in the application of formal and moral criteria.
- A separation between the 'is' and the 'ought' is useful in providing a standard by which positive law can be evaluated and criticised. Even naturalists concede that there will always be some discrepancy between law as it is and as it ought to be, and as long as this is so, the latter can be used to evaluate the former.

The above is an attempt to clarify what is perhaps the most important contention of contemporary positivism and this argument is not conclusive. In considering positivist theories it should not be forgotten that although there is value in identifying laws clearly for practical purposes, there is more value to moral or natural principles than what they have attached to such notions.

****

Custom as a Source of Law in India

(Abstract based on the Article of M.P. J a i n)

In any scheme of teaching Jurisprudence custom has an important place as a source of law. There is, however, a rich material in Indian social and legal history which can more appropriately be made use of in explaining the place of custom in society.

- **Western Jurists:-** In the evolution of the human society, it appears to be beyond doubt that custom arose first, law came later. Customs arise whenever a few human beings come together, as no association of human beings can exist permanently without adopting consciously or unconsciously, some definite rules governing reciprocal rights and obligations. Even a primitive tribe may have a legal order long before it has developed a state. It also looks to be axiomatic that, to start with, law was built upon custom.
  - Custom is regarded as a source of law by the Western jurists, though they assign importance to it to a varying degree depending upon their approach and outlook. Austin having defined 'law' as the command of a political superior or definite human authority addressed to political inferiors and enforced by a penalty or sanction, held that custom becomes a law only when it receives judicial or legislative recognition.
- Holland, though practically adopting Austin's definition of law, nevertheless, holds that custom was law before it received the stamp of judicial authentication. Allen also disagrees with Austin's thesis. He regards custom as "self-contained, self-sufficient, and self-justified law" and says that the function of the court is "declaratory rather than constitutive".
- The Historical Jurists held that all early law was customary, and that the function of legislation is limited to supplementing and redefining custom. According to Savigny, the real bases of all positive law is to be found in the general consciousness of people (Volksgeist). The source of law is not the command of the sovereign, not even the habits of a community, but the 'instinctive sense of right possessed by every race'. Custom is thus evidence of law whose real source lies deeper in the minds of men.
- To Puchta, custom was only self-sufficient and independent of legislative authority but was a condition precedent, of all sound legislation. Of course, the flaw in this theory is that there are customs which are not based on an instinctive sense of right in the community as a whole, but on the interests of a strong minority, for example, slavery.
  - In India; here for long before the advent of the British, customs were observed by the people, and were enforced not by the courts but by the village or community panchayats; the Government did not interfere with the prevalent norms. When the British system of Justice came, these very customs came to be pleaded before the courts which enforced them.
- **Hindu View of Custom:-** Custom has always been given a very important place as a source of law by the Hindu Jurists. Two views have prevailed regarding the relative value of custom vis-a-vis the sruti and smriti. The Dharmashastra writers subordinated customs to sruti and smriti which were given a higher authority. Thus, according to Gautam, dharmas

(customs) of countries, castes and families, which are not opposed to Vedic scriptures, are authoritative and binding.

- Manu and Yajnavalkya declare that sources of Dharma are sruti, smriti and sadachara in that order. Mitakshara, Dayabhaga, Mayukha also place custom as subordinate to sruti and smriti. Some of the smritis underlined the significance of customs by saying that suppression of customs would give rise to resentment and rebellion.
  - The Arthasastra writer, Kautilya, held that usages and customs were of equal authority as evidence of law; and in case of conflict between them, the former must be taken to be of greater force as being actually observed in practice.
  - It may also be pointed out that while customs were recognized, it would also be correct to say that customs also, to some extent, were modified and supplemented by the opinions of the Hindu Jurists. In Sanskrit, the word for custom is sadachara.
- **Muslim View of Custom:-** The two principal sources of the Islamic law are the Koran, as containing the word of God, and the hadis or traditions, being the inspired utterances of the Prophet and precedents derived from his acts. Next important sources are : ijma, the consensus of opinion amongst the learned; urf or custom; and qiyas, the analogical deductions from the first three.

- Prophet Mohamed himself recognized the force of customary law. He either gave his express sanction to certain pre-Islamic usages prevalent amongst the Arabs, or suffered such usages to continue without expressing disapprobation. His companions, after his death, recognized many customs which were not inconsistent with the teaching of the Islamic faith. The hadis contained, to a large extent, the customary law of pre- Islamic Arabia. It is thus clear that in its formative stages the Muslim law drew a good deal from the customs prevailing in Arabia.
- Hence, according to the strict rule of Muslim law, a custom opposed to the principles derived from the former sources is illegal. The conditions laid down for the validity of custom, under the Muslim law are : first, it must be generally prevalent in the country; second, it must not be merely a local usage in a village or a town; third, it must be an established course of conduct, and, fourth, custom being essentially territorial, it cannot affect the law in other lands, and as it is confined to a particular period it cannot affect the custom in another age.
- **Custom in the Modern Indian Legal System:-** The Englishmen were very particular in leaving the personal laws of the people undisturbed as much as possible and this attitude characterized the whole of the British period. The adalats system created by Warren Hastings in Bengal, Bihar and Orissa were directed to decide all cases of inheritance, marriage, caste and other religious usages and institutions according to the laws of the Koran with respect to the Muhammadans and the laws of the Shastras with respect to the Hindus.
- Further, in the Madras Civil Courts Act, 1873, it was laid down that to decide any question regarding succession, inheritance, marriage or caste, or religious institution, "the Muhammadan law...and the Hindu law..., any custom (if such there be) having the force of law and governing the parties or property concerned, shall form the rule of decision "

- However, the above actions did not follow a uniform pattern insofar as the question of the relative position of custom vis-a-vis the personal law was concerned. Insofar as the Hindus were concerned, the courts, took note of the great importance given to custom in the ancient India, by maintaining that clear proof of usage will outweigh the written text of the law. This judicial approach to custom in the area of Hindu law, even though not in conformity with the orthodox approach, was yet in conformity with the genius of the law which always gave a high regard to custom.
- The position of custom in the area of Muslim law remained doubtful for quite some time. and traditionally, the Muslim Jurists placed custom at a low level of priority. Courts did not always adopt the text of the Koran as law any further than it has been adopted in the customs and usages of the Muhammadans.
- As an example of interdependence of religious customs, on the coast of Malabar in Kerala, people known as Mopalas, who are Muslims by religion, follow not the orthodox system of Muslim law but the Hindu law known as Marumukkthayam or matriarchal system and their customs have been applied by the courts. custom.
- Thus, in India "custom played a large part in modifying the ordinary law. in deciding questions regarding succession, marriage, special property of women, betrothal, divorce, dower, adoption, guardianship, minority, bastardy, family relations, wills, legacies, gifts, partitions of any religious usage or institution, custom was thus made the first rule of decision.
- **Kinds of Customs Enforced:-** Thus, it is clear that during the British Period, the customs came to be given a pre-eminent place as a rule of decision. This happened as a result of statutory provisions, or where these were deficient, by the judicial interpretation. The courts accepted and applied customs of all types, e.g., tribal, communal, sectarian, local, family etc.
- Most of the customs brought before the courts are tribal, communal or sectarian. For example, the Kamma community in Andhra has a custom of affiliating a son-in-law and giving him a share in the property; this adoption known as illatom adoption has been recognized by the Court. Nairs in South Malabar have peculiar usages. Some of them have been judicially established. Amongst them, polyandry was legally recognized, and descent of property was through females.
- A family custom is one which applies to a particular family only. In a number of cases, too many to recount here, family customs have been applied by the courts. An interesting institution created by custom, which was recognized and prevalent

among certain families in certain parts of the country, is that of a 'composite family', i.e., two or more families agree to live and work together, pool their resources, shoulder the common risks, utilize the resources indiscriminately for the purposes of the whole family. Patna High Court disagrees with this view.

- **Requisites of a Valid Custom:-** A custom is a rule which in a particular family or in a particular district, has, from long usage, obtained the force of law. A custom to be legally recognizable and enforceable must fulfill several requisites, viz., it must be ancient, certain and reasonable, and must be construed strictly.

- A custom to be valid must be ancient. The Royal Court in England laid down the rule that country custom was only valid if immemorial. All that is necessary to prove is that the usage has been acted upon in practice for such a long period and with such invariability as to show that it has, by common consent, been submitted to as the established governing rule of a particular locality. Hindu legislations say 'for a long period' instead of 'immemorial', which denotes that the English rule has not been adopted.
  - A custom should not be unreasonable. It should not be against reason, but the reason referred to here "is not to be understood as meaning every unlearned man's reason but artificial and legal reason warranted by authority of law". For example, a right of passage over the land of another may be regarded as unreasonable if it completely deprives the owner of his right to the lands. its basis.
  - A custom should not be immoral or opposed to public policy or against justice, equity and good sense. Some customs regarding divorce have been held to be immoral; a custom permitting a woman to desert her husband at her pleasure and marry again without his consent, a custom by which the marriage tie could be dissolved by either husband or wife against the wish of the divorced party on payment of a sum of money etc. A custom abhorrent to decency or morality however long practiced and recognized by a community cannot be enforced by the courts. Thus a custom permitting marriage with daughter's daughter was held immoral.
- **Proof of a Custom:-** Before the advent of the British period, the customs of the people were mostly unwritten and unrecorded and were enshrined in the "unexpressed consciousness of the people' and were enforced by the village panchayats. However, later on, it became necessary to ascertain the customs and record them in writing.
- The first important principle laid down by the courts in a large number of cases is that a party alleging that he is governed by a custom must specifically allege the same and prove its existence. The custom must be established by clear and unambiguous proof, by satisfactory evidence. In the absence of such an evidence the court cannot come to a conclusion whether any custom is really operative or what is its content and scope.
- Decisions of courts regarding a custom are relevant under S. 42 of the Indian Evidence Act, though under that section they are not conclusive. It has been held again and again that where a custom is repeatedly brought to the notice of the courts, the courts may hold that custom was introduced into the law and that no further proof was necessary of the custom in each case. Therefore, a custom by repeated recognition by courts becomes entitled to judicial notice.
- **Abrogation of Custom:-** While it was the settled policy of the British administration to preserve customs of the people in the administration of justice, there were certain forces which were working for their abrogation. One such effort, on a very big scale, was made through the Muslim Shari at Act, 1937, which abrogated customs applicable to Muhammadans and restored them to their personal law specially in matters related to marriage, dissolution of marriage, maintenance, dower, guardianship, gifts, trust and trust property etc. which condemned the customary law as adversely affecting their rights.

- With a view to introducing uniformity in, and to liberalize, the law applicable to the Hindus, certain portions of it have been codified recently. By far and large, the effect of this legislation has been to reduce the importance of custom though it is not correct to say that custom has been completely abrogated. Some force is still given to customary law. abrogated. Section 4 of the Hindu Succession Act, 1956, provides for the overriding effect of the Act in respect of matters dealt with by it. Any custom inconsistent with it is abrogated.

- A large volume of case-law arose in India having a bearing on custom. Custom came to play a very important part as a source of law; it took a place second only to the statutory law; custom was given preference over the religious laws of the parties. It was only just and equitable that the customs which people had been observing in practice be enforced rather than the theoretical law contained in the books.

- In India, some of the family customs too came to be fully recognized and enforced. Similarly, the communal or tribal customs were enforced, whereas such would not be the case in England. It may be noted that a large mass of custom here is tribal or sectarian.

- In England, the term 'usage' is used for a general line of conduct adopted by persons in a particular department of business life. In India, the term 'usage' has been accepted by the courts as having nothing to do with trade or commerce but covered all aspects of family relations. There is a great difference between a 'custom' and 'usage' and that clearly the latter may be established in a much less period of time than a custom.

- Another doctrine adopted in India, for which no parallel can be found in England, is that a family can renounce customs applicable to it and adopt other customs. Rather than resort to principles borrowed from a foreign Jurisprudence and unknown to people, it was considered better to enforce such customs as were observed and recognized domestically. Though Hindu law has been codified and reformed and made uniform throughout the country, certain customs have been still preserved even at the cost of uniformity.

- It appears that customs have had their heyday and they have practically exhausted their efficacy as law-creating agency. They have now ceased to act as a fruitful agency of law reform. New customs are difficult to get recognition from the courts. The future legal growth in India will be mostly due to legislation, and to some extent, judicial interpretation and precedent. Custom is useful for situations which have already occurred, but cannot create a rule to deal with a future difficulty.

- The predominance of custom makes the system less uniform; it varies from family to family, from region to region and from community to community. It places a double burden on the judiciary which has to decide not only questions of fact, but also to take evidence to decide existence and content of the custom alleged to be applicable to the facts.

- As time passes on, custom is bound to lose its pre-eminent position which it has enjoyed so long in India. It was inevitable till the legal system itself was in its formative stages. But when the legal system has achieved maturity, people have also become sophisticated and literate and, therefore, time is ripe for uniform legislation and abolition of custom. In every mature and developed system, custom plays a very minor role.

* * * * * *

Ancient, Customary and Codified Laws, an Analysis

(Abstract of M.D.A. Freeman, *Lloyd's Introduction to Jurisprudence*)

TheConceptof*Themistes*

Historical Materialism underscores the belief that the progress of mankind in almost all the disciplines was the product of a historical evolution tilted more towards the material origin of jurisprudence rejecting the so called divine oligarchic legal structure.

"Themis,"as it is well known, appears in the later Greek system as the Goddess of Justice, and 'Themistes' believed in the divine origin of juristic knowledge and authority. Throughout the evolution of mankind, conventional jurists were inclined to lay down a priori that the notion of a custom must precede that of a judicial sentence, and that a judgment must affirm a custom or punish its breach, as it seemed certain that the basic notion is a historical order of the ideas.

- *Customary Law-* The important point for the jurist is that aristocracies were universally the depositaries and administrators of law. They seem to have succeeded to the prerogatives of the king, who claim a divine origin for the entire body of rules, or for certain parts of it. Before the invention of writing, and during the infancy of the art, an aristocracy invested with judicial privileges formed the legal frame.
  - The epoch of Customary Law, and of its custody by a privileged order, is a very remarkable one. The law, thus known exclusively to a privileged minority, whether a caste, an aristocracy or a priestly tribe, is true unwritten law. The elder English judges did really pretend to knowledge or rules, principles, and distinctions which were not entirely revealed to the bar and to the lay-public.
- However, such legal principles presently ceased to be unwritten law. As soon as the Courts at Westminster Hall began to base their judgments on cases recorded, whether in the year- books or elsewhere, the law which they administered became written law. It is written case- law, and only different from code-law because it is written in a different way.
  - From the period of Customary Law we come to another sharply defined era of Codes, where laws engraven on tablets and published to the people take the place of usages deposited with the recollection of a privileged oligarchy. Inscribed codes were seen to be a better depository of law, and a better security for its accurate preservation, than the memory of a number of persons however strengthened by habitual exercise.
- The movement of the progressive societies has been uniform in one respect. The difficulty to see what is the tie between man and man was replaced by the discussion over the reciprocity of rights and duties which have their origin in the Family. Starting, as from one terminus of history, from a condition of society in which all the relations of Persons are summed up in the relations of Family, we seem to have steadily moved towards a phase of social order in which discourse over rights and duties gained prominence.

Through the steady growth of jurisprudential thinking and writing, the word Status which was primarily individual has given way to interpersonal legal discourse which has been a movement from Status to Contract.

******

Historical and Anthropological Approaches

(Extract taken from R.W.M. Dias' writings on *Jurisprudence*)

The historical approach to jurisprudence comprises on inquiries into the past and evolution generally with the object of elucidating the position today. Another type of inquiries into the past, especially into primitive and undeveloped communities, also were conducted for their own sake in order to discover what 'law' meant to humans anthropologically and such inquiries are distinguishable as the Anthropological approach.

- Historical School:- The Historical School proclaimed that law is the story of the study and reception of Roman law in

Europe. With the dissolution of the Roman Empire, there was a revival of academic interest in that system in the eleventh century in France and Italy. Gradually this paved the way for the later reception of Roman law into Europe in the fifteenth and sixteenth centuries in a diluted manner.

- ◦ The Renaissance kindled fresh interest in the teachings of the Romans themselves. The outstanding name in this connection is that of Cujas, a Frenchman, who was the first scholar to understand Justinian's Corpus Juris in historical perspective. The admirable work of Cujas, however, was confined to the academic sphere and failed to penetrate through to practice. Accordingly, there developed a gulf between the academic jurist and the practitioner in the historical approach.
- ◦ The position of Germany at the start of the nineteenth century deserves special mention, since this was the cradle of the Historical School. Thibaut, of Heidelberg, in 1814 for suggested for a code on the lines of the Code Napoleon. However, the move towards codification was effectively halted and it was after many years of sustained agitation, in 1900 that Germany ultimately acquired her code, the Biirgerliches Gesetzbuch.
- ◦ As opposed to the naturalists' automatic derivation of law from nature, the historical thinkers argued for a realistic investigation into historical truths. This was a factor which weighed heavily with Savigny, a conservative nobleman, who acquired a deep and lasting hatred for violent reforms. With the French conquests under Napoleon aroused the nationalism of Europe, the French had spread the idea of codified law, and the reaction against anything French carried with it hostility to codification.
- ◦ Montesquieu had maintained that law was shaped by social, geographical and historical considerations; Burke in England had voiced the same sentiment by pointing to the importance of tradition as a guide to social change. These factors, boosted by the genius of Savigny, started European thought along a new road.
- ◦ Savigny's interest in historical studies has appeared in 1803 in his first major work, "Das Recht des Bestizes" (The Law of Possession). He set himself the task of laying the foundation for future historical labours by producing a basic history of the development of Roman law in medieval Europe. In his great work, "The History of Roman Law in the Middle Ages", he analysed the Roman element to its roots, and in another text, "The System of Modern Roman Law", he analysed Roman and local laws. Historical research was according to him, the indispensable means to the understanding and reform of the present, and he said;

"The existing matter will be injurious to us so long as we ignorantly submit to it; but beneficial if we oppose to it a vivid creative energy — obtain the mastery over it by a thorough grounding in history and thus appropriate to ourselves the whole intellectual wealth of preceding generations" [Savigny Introduction to The System of Modern Roman Law].

- ◦ The nature of any particular system of law, he said, was a reflection of the spirit of the people, who evolved it. This was later characterised as the Volksgeist by Puchta, Savigny's most devoted disciple. All law, according to him, is the manifestation of this common consciousness. He wrote;

"Law grows with the growth, and strengthens with the strength of the people, and finally dies away as the nation loses its nationality" [Puchta, Outlines of the Science of Jurisprudence].

- ◦ A nation, to Savigny, meant only a community of people linked together by historical, geographical and cultural ties. He then went on to elaborate the theory of the Volksgeist by contending that it is the broad principles of the system that are to be found in the spirit of the people. In place of the moral authority, claimed by the natural lawyers, the Historical School substituted social pressure. This view of Savigny's historical method of work, leads to the following points on the idea of Volksgeist;

1. The idea of the Volksgeist certainly suited the mood of the German people but limited too. It was a time of the growing sense of nationhood and a desire for unification. It would appear that Savigny's historical sense to some extent deserted him, for it amounts, in effect, to the adoption of an a priori preconception. It seemed that he too had attempted to draw an inference from limited data.

2. Savigny's endeavour to establish that the reception of Roman law had taken place so long ago as to make it acceptable by Germanic Volksgeist was unconvincing. The reception of English law in so many parts of the world is also evidence of supra-national adaptability and resilience going beyond spirit of specific societies.

3. The Volksgeist theory minimises the influence which individuals, sometimes of alien race, have exercised upon legal development. Every man is a product of his time, but occasionally there are men who by their genius are able to give legal development new directions.

4. The influence of the Volksgeist is at most only a limited one. The national character of law seems to manifest itself more strongly in some branches than in others, for example, in family law rather than in commercial or criminal law. Thus, the general reception of Roman law in Europe did not include Roman family law. Even more significant is the fact that the successful introduction of alien systems into countries like India affected the indigenous family laws least of all.

5. Law is sometimes used deliberately to change existing ideas; and it may also be used to further inter-state co-operation in many spheres. Even in

Germany one may instance Bismarck's shrewd and successful attempt to go beyond the German Volksgeist by introducing some special laws to deal with the socialist movements.

6. Many institutions have originated, not in a Volksgeist, but in the convenience of a ruling oligarchy, e.g. slavery.

7. Many customs owe their origin to the force of imitation rather than to any innate conviction of their righteousness.

8. Some rules of customary law may not reflect the spirit of the whole population, e.g. local customs. The question is: if law is the product of a Volksgeist, how is it that only some people and not all have evolved a special rule? In such an analysis, it is not at all clear who the Volk are whose Geist determines the law.

9. Important rules of law sometimes develop as the result of conscious and violent struggle between conflicting interests within the nation, and not as a result of mutual growth, e.g. the law relating to trade unions and industry.

10. A different objection to the Volksgeist came from Savigny's opponents. They pointed out that, taken literally, his thesis would deter the unification of Germany permanently by emphasising the individuality of

each separate state and by fostering a narrow sense of nationalism.

11. An inconsistency in Savigny's work was that, while he was the protagonist of the Volksgeist doctrine, he worked at the same time for the acceptance of a purified Roman law as the law of Germany. Far from the law being a reflection of the Volksgeist, it would seem that the Volksgeist had been shaped by the law.

2. Savigny's veneration for Roman law led him to advance certain dubious propositions. For instance, there was in Roman law a strict adherence to the doctrine of privity of contract with few exceptions, i.e. no one other than parties to a contract can be entitled or obliged under it. The law of negotiable instruments, of course, is a contradiction of this. Savigny accordingly condemned negotiable instruments as 'logically impossible.' Indeed, the crucial weakness of Savigny's approach was that he venerated past institutions without regard to their suitability to the present.

3. Savigny's thesis, however, contained another and even more awkward implication. The only persons who talked of the Volksgeist were academic jurists, unversed in the practical problems of legal administration. Therefore, the Volksgeist resolved itself into what these theorists imagined it to be.

4. Consistently with this theory, Savigny further maintained that legislation was subordinate to custom. It should at all times conform to the Volksgeist. Reform in his view, should await the results of the historians' work. Savigny's work, on the whole, was a salutary corrective to the methods of the natural lawyers.

5. Another writer of whom some mention should be made is Gierke who authored "Natural Law and the Theory of Society". He proceeded to trace the progress of social and legal

development in the form of a history of the law and practice of associations and individuals. In his view legal and social history is most accurately portrayed as a perpetual struggle between the Genossenshaft (fraternal collaboration of people) and the Herrschaft (the idea of domination by the state).

Factually speaking, historic approach did not succeed in reconciling the issues involved in the positivist and naturalist schools. However, the expression of reason and the sense of right promoted by the historical school gained importance in the further development of world jurisprudence.

The Anthropological Approach

Anthropological investigations into the nature of primitive and undeveloped systems of law are of modern origin and might be regarded as a product of the Historical School. This movement was pioneered by Sir Henry Maine who was the first and the greatest representative of the historical movement in England. He began his work with a mass of material already published on the history and development of Roman law by the German Historical School. Instead of stressing the uniqueness of national institutions, he brought to bear a scientific urge to unify, classify and generalise the evolution of different legal orders.

- Maine was led to distinguish between what he called 'static' and 'progressive' societies which travel in his thesis, into four stages. The first stage is that of law-making by personal command, believed to be of divine inspiration. The second stage occurs when those commands crystallise into customs. In the third stage the ruler is superseded by a minority who obtain control over the law. The fourth stage is the revolt of the majority against this oligarchic monopoly, and the publication of the law in the form of a code.
- 'Static, societies, according to Maine, do not progress beyond the above point. The characteristic feature of 'progressive' societies is that they proceed to develop the law by three methods - fiction, equity and legislation. He recognised that the advance of civilisation demanded an increasing use of legislation, and he often contended that the confused state of English law was due to its pre-eminently judge-made character. He also did not share Savigny's mystique of the Volkgeist.
- According to Maine, the legal condition of the individual is determined by status, i.e. his claims, duties, liberties etc. which are determined by law. He maintained that the movement of progressive societies has been a movement from Status (determined by law) to Contract (determined by individual free will).
- During the time of Maine, the study of anthropology has developed into a separate branch of learning. Maine's age was one in which legislation was removing the disabilities of Catholics, Jews, Dissenters and married women. He witnessed the triumph in the American Civil War of the North, a community based on contract, over the feudal and status-regulated South.
  - In the modern age, however, a return to status has been detected. In public affairs, and in industry in particular, the individual is no longer able to negotiate his own terms. This is the age of the standardised contract, and of collective bargaining.
- It is now thought that there were seven grades of primitive societies, the First and Second Hunters, the First, Second and Third Agricultural Grades, and the First and Second Pastoral Grades. The agricultural and pastoral grades are to some

extent parallel. The degree of development of social institutions does bear some correspondence with the degree of economic development.

- Critics of Maine held that primitive law was by no means as rigid as Maine had supposed, nor were people inflexibly bound by it. It is generally agreed that even in primitive societies people do control their destinies, that they are by no means blindly subservient to custom.
- Diamond criticises Maine most strongly for his assertion that law and religion were indistinguishable. Hoebel, on the other hand, defends Maine on this point. Bohannan has suggested that law comes into being when customary reciprocal obligations become further institutionalised in a way that society continues to function on the basis of rules.
- According to Hocrat the means by which primitive societies sought life was ritual. The lives and well-being of individuals depended on the life and well-being of society. Ritual was therefore a social affair and society had to organise itself for it. The structure of ritual was such that different rules were assigned to different individuals and groups. In all this one may detect the origin of caste; the various castes that one finds, the fisher, the farmer, the launderer, the potter, etc.
- It is believed that the king being identified with nature, the prosperity of the people could only be achieved by making the king prosperous. Revenue and tribute were the means of making him so.

Anthropological enquiries stress one thing which is endorsed by the proponents that primitive law is prescriptive in nature and function. Even though, it was considered to be an extension of the historical school the anthropological approach was critical of the historical jurisprudence when ever required.

* * * * *

Roscoe Pound and the Social Engineering Theory*

Abstract based on R.W.M. Dias' writings on **Jurisprudence**

In America, the law school and the jurist enjoy a status superior to that of their counterparts in Great Britain. These factors have combined to produce an American movement in sociological jurisprudence lead by Roscoe Pound of the Harvard Law School.

- Sociological jurisprudence, according to Pound, should ensure that the making, interpretation and application of laws take account of social facts. Towards achieving this end there should be;

a. A factual study of the social effects of legal administration,
b. Social investigations as preliminaries to legislation,
c. A constant study of the means for making laws more effective, which involves,
d. The study, both psychological and philosophical, of the judicial method,
e. A sociological study of legal history,
f. Allowance for the possibility of a just and reasonable solution of individual cases,
g. A ministry of justice in English-speaking countries, and
h. The achievement of the purposes of the various laws.

- So in order to achieve the purposes of the legal order, in the words of Pound, there has to be;

  a. A recognition of certain interests, individual, public and social,
  b. A definition of the limits within which such interests will be legally recognised and given effect to, and
  c. The securing of those interests within the limits as defined.

- When determining the scope and subject-matter of the system, the following five things require to be done;

  a. Preparation of an inventory of interests, classifying them;

  ii. Selection of the interests which should be legally recognised;
  iii. Demarcation of the limits of securing the interests so selected;
  iv. Consideration of the means whereby laws might secure the interests when these have been acknowledged and delimited; and
  v. Evolution of the principles of valuation of the interests.

- Pound likened the task of the lawyer to engineering, an analogy which he used repeatedly. The aim of social engineering is to build as efficient a structure of society as possible, which requires the satisfaction of the maximum of wants with

- R.W.M. Dias, *Jurisprudence*, 431-35 (1985).

the minimum of friction and waste. It involves the balancing of competing interests. Pound's arrangement of these, elaborated in detail, was as follows:

- Individual Interests. These are claims or demands or desires involved in and looked at from the standpoint of the individual life. They concern:-

1. *Personality*. This includes interests in (a) the physical person, (b) freedom of will, (c) honour and reputation, (d) privacy, and (e) belief and opinion.
2. *Domestic relations*. It is important to distinguish between the interest of individuals in domestic relationships and that of society in such institutions as family and marriage. Individual interests include those of

   a. parents, (b) children, (c) husbands, and (d) wives.

3. *Interest of substance*. This includes interests of (a) property, (b) freedom of industry and contract, (c) promised advantages, (d) advantageous relations with others, (e) freedom of association, and (f) continuity of employment.

- Public Interests. These are claims or demands or desires asserted by individuals in title of a politically organised society which are mainly of two types;

1. *Interests of the state as a juristic person.* These, include (a) the integrity, freedom of action and honour of the state's personality, and (b)

claims of the politically organised society as a corporation to property

acquired and held for corporate purposes.

2. *Interests of the state as guardian of social interests.* This concept is explained in the next major category.

- Social Interests. These are claims or demands or desires, even some of the foregoing in other aspects, thought of in terms of social life and generalised as claims of the social group and include;

1. *Social interest in the general security–* This is the claim of the civilised society to be secured against those forms of action and courses of conduct which threaten its existence which relate to (a) general safety, (b) general health, (c) peace and order, (d) security of acquisitions, and (e) security of transactions.
2. *Socialinterestinthesecurityofsocialinstitutions.*This is the claim of the civilised society that its fundamental institutions be secured from factors which threaten their existence or impair their efficient functioning and comprises of (a) domestic institutions, (b) religious institutions, (c) political institutions, and (d) economic institutions.
3. *Socialinterestingeneralmorals.*This is the of the civilised society to be secured against factors offensive to the moral sentiments of it and conveys a variety of laws, for example, those dealing with prostitution, drunkenness and gambling.

4. *Social interest in the conservation of social resources.* This is the claim of the civilised society that the goods of existence shall not be wasted and covers (a) conservation of natural resources, and (b) conservation of human resources.
5. *Social interest in general progress–* This is the claim of the civilised society that the goods of existence shall not be wasted; which has three aspects;

   a. Economic progress, which covers (i) freedom of use and sale of property, (ii) free trade, (iii) free industry, and (iv) encouragement of invention by the grant of patents.
   b. Political progress, which covers (i) free speech, and (ii) free associations; and
   c. cultural progress, which covers (i) free science, (ii) free letters, (iii) free arts, (iv) promotion of education and learning, and (v) aesthetics.

6. *Social interest in individual life.* This is the claim or of the civilised society that each individual be able to live a human life therein according to the standards of the society and involves (a) self-assertion, (b) opportunity, and (c) conditions of life.

- Pound maintains that one cannot balance an individual interest against a social interest.

He classifies the institutions of the law as follows. There are, first, rules, which are precepts attaching definite consequences to definite factual situations. Secondly, there are principles, which are authoritative points of departure for legal reasoning in cases not covered by rules. Thirdly, there are conceptions, which are categories to which types or classes of transactions and situations can be referred and on the basis of which a set of rules, principles or standards becomes applicable. Fourthly, there are doctrines, which are the union of rules, principles and conceptions with regard to particular situations or types of cases in logically independent schemes so that reasoning may proceed on the basis of the scheme and its logical implications. Finally, there are standards prescribing the limits of permissible conduct, which are to be applied according to the circumstances of each case.

- Pound assumes that 'Recognition' has many gradations, which makes it necessary to specify in what sense an interest is recognised as such. It is not interests as such, but the yardsticks with reference to which they are measured that matter. Whether the proprietary right of a slave-owner is to be upheld or not depends upon whether sanctity of property or sanctity of the person is adopted as the ideal. The choice of an ideal, or even a choice between competing ideals, is a matter of decision, not of balancing.

- The 'weight' to be attached to an interest will vary according to the ideal that is used. The point is that the whole idea of balancing is subordinate to the ideal that is in view. The march of society is marked by changes in its ideals and standards for measuring interests.

- In any case, all questions of interests and ideals should be considered in the context of particular issues as and when they come up for decision. It is for the judge to translate the activity involved in the case before him in terms of an interest and to select the ideal with reference to which the competing interests are to be measured.
  - The recognition of a new interest is a matter of policy. Interests need only be considered as and when they arise in disputes; the matter that is of importance is the way in which they are viewed and evaluated by the particular judge.
- In any case, lists of interests are only the products of personal opinion. Different writers have presented them differently. As Pound himself says, in most cases it is preferable to transfer individual interests on to the plane of social interests when considering them. It is the ideal with reference to which any interest is considered that matters, not so much the interest itself.
  - Critics of Roscoe Pound argue that it is difficult to see how the balancing of interests will produce a cohesive society where there are minorities whose interests are irreconcilable with those of the majority. There is a different problem where a substantial proportion of the populace is parochially minded and have little or no sense of nationhood.

Thus, even though, the social engineering theory had marked an era of change in modern jurisprudence, it is worth while repeating that Pound seems to have devoted too little attention in developing a mechanism of evaluation for rights. It is submitted by his critics that it would have been preferable had he enlarged on the criteria of evaluating interests instead of developing particular interests.

* * * * *

Legal Service, Legal Aid and Lok Adalat

(Abstract based on the Writings of R. Swaroop)

There could not be any real equality in criminal cases unless the accused got a fair trial of defending himself against the charges laid and unless he had competent professional assistance. In *Hussainara Khatoon v. State of Bihar* [AIR 1979 SC 1369, 1375], the Supreme Court observed that it was not possible to reach the benefits of the legal process to the poor, to protect them against injustice and to secure to them their constitutional and statutory rights unless there was a nationwide legal service programme to provide free legal services to them. The Supreme court observed:

"Today, unfortunately, in our country the poor are priced out of the judicial system with the result that they are losing faith in the capacity of our legal system to bring about changes in their life conditions and to deliver justice to them. The result is that the legal system has lost its credibility for the weaker sections of the community. It is, therefore, necessary that we should inject equal justice into legality and that can be done only by dynamic and activism scheme of legal services. That is not only a mandate of equal justice implicit in Article 14 and right to life and liberty conferred by Article 21, but also the compulsion of the Constitutional Directive embodied in Article 39-A."

- It is also the constitutional obligation of the Court, as the guardian of the fundamental rights of the people, to enforce the fundamental right of the accused to fair trial and his right to free legal aid or to secure assistance of a counsel, where he cannot afford to engage one, on account of indigence or poverty.
- In India, less than 33 percent of the people know how to write and read sufficiently and usefully and majority of the people are poor or indigent and most of them live below the poverty line, even though poverty line is drawn liberally, and not upon an International Standard.
- It is therefore, imperative to reach the goal of 'equal access to justice,' which is a constitutional commandment and statutory imperative. It is in this context, the provisions for legal services have been made in the Constitution as well as in the Legal Services Authorities Act, 1987, over and above the provisions made in Section 304 of the Criminal Procedure Code, 1973.
- As pointed out by the Court in *Rhem v. Malcolm* [377 F. Supp. 995]: "the law does not permit any Government to deprive its citizens of constitutional rights on a plan of poverty" and to quote the words of Justice Black mum in *Jackson v. Bishop* [404 F Supp 2d, 571]: "human considerations and constitutional requirements are not in this day to be measured by dollar considerations" (*Khatri v. State of Bihar*, AIR 1981 SC 928, 930).
- *Constitutional Mandate*- The Founding Fathers of the Constitution of India have taken a positive approach of doctrine of philosophy of Equal Justice which was promised in the preamble of the Constitution. The preamble promise is further strengthened by

the constitutional provisions in Articles 14, 19, 21, 22(1), 32, 39-A, 51-A and 226 of the Constitution of India.

- Article 22(1) of the Constitution, expressly provides that, "No person, who is arrested, shall be detained in custody, without being informed, as soon as may be, of the grounds for such arrest, nor shall he be denied of the right to consult and to be defended by a legal practitioner of his choice."
- Long before the Constitution, even in the Old Criminal Procedure Code, under Section 340(1), it had been provided that: "Any person, accused of an offence before the Criminal Court or against whom proceedings are instituted, under this Code, or any such Code, may of right, be defended by a pleader" and Section 303 of the new Code corresponds to the said section, with the addition of the words 'of his choice' at the end.
- *Free legal services an essential element of fair procedure*- It was explained in [*Maneka Gandhi v. Union of India*, AIR 1978 SC 597] that the procedure established by law under Article 21 of the Constitution of India under which a person may be deprived of his life or liberty should be 'reasonable', fair. One can add that a procedure which does not make legal services available to an accused person cannot possibly be regarded as 'reasonable, fair and just.'
- *Insertion of Article 39A providing for equal justice and free legal aid -As a principle of policy to be followed by the State:* The Constitution (Forty-second

Amendment) Act, 1976 has inserted Article 39-A as a Directive Principle of State Policy.

This Article stipulates that –

Article-39-A- *Equal justice and free legal aid* – "The State shall secure that the operation of the legal system promotes justice, on the basis of equal opportunity and shall, in particular, provide free legal aid, by suitable legislation or schemes or in any other way, to ensure that opportunities for securing justice are not denied to any citizen by reason of economic or other disabilities".

- In *SukhDasv. Union Territory of Arunachal Pradesh,* the Supreme Court while interpreting legal aid as a fundamental right which the state is constitutionally obliged to provide to every indigent accused in criminal proceedings, that this fundamental right could not be denied to the accused if they did not apply for free legal aid.
- In *Khatri v. State of Bihar,* the Supreme Court has held thus:-The right to free legal aid extends not only at the stage of trial but also at the stage when an accused is first produced before the Magistrate or the Sessions Judge who must be held to be under an obligation to inform the accused that if he is unable to engage the services of a lawyer on account of poverty or indigence, he is entitled to obtain free legal services at the cost of the State.
- *Reports of Law Commission of India- Right to be provided with a lawyer by theState-*For the first time it was in the year 1958, the Law Commission of India in its Fourteenth Report observed, - "Unless some provision is made for assisting the poor man for the payment of court-fees and lawyer's fees and other incidental costs of litigation, he/she is denied equality in the opportunity to seek justice."

- Again in 1969 the 41st Law Commission Report, the Law Commission strongly recommended that representation by a lawyer should be made available at Government expenses to accused persons in all cases tried by a Court of Sessions. The Law Commission in its Forty Eighth Report also suggested for making provision for free legal assistance by the State for all accused who were undefended by a lawyer for want of means.
- *Recommendation codified in Section 304 CrPC-* This recommendation has now been codified in sub-section (1) of Section 304 of the Code of Criminal Procedure, with this change made by the Joint Committee, that the State aid will be available only where the accused "has not sufficient means to engage a pleader".
- In *RajKishorev.State,* AIR 1969 Cal 321, the court held "while, it is settled position of law that to provide legal aid to accused persons without means in all cases tried by a Court of Session, is a mandatory constitutional necessity, it is further necessary that such lawyer should be of competence. Such counsel appointed for the accused must be given the complete brief of the case and time to prepare the case. Failure to this is a denial of proper representation of the accused and vitiates the trial.
- *Committee for Implementing Legal Aid Scheme (CILAS) -* In September, 1980, the Government of India, with the object of providing free legal aid, appointed "Committee for Implementing Legal Aid Schemes" (CILAS) with P.N. Bhagwati J (as he then was) as the Chairman to monitor and implement legal aid programs on a uniform basis in all the States and union territories.
- The Legal Services Authorities act, 1987- This law was enacted with a view to constitute Legal Services Authorities at National, State and District Levels which was brought into force with effect from 09-11-1995, almost eight years after its enactment.
- *Constitution of Legal Aid Boards and Committees-* For effective implementation and to achieve the desired objective of providing Free Legal Aid and Advice to the poor, State Boards, District Legal Aid Committees and Taluk Committees were constituted.
  - *Need for Strategic Legal Aid Programme-*Strategic legal aid programme consisting of promotion of legal literacy, organization of legal aid camps, encouragement of public interest litigation and holding of Lok adalats or niti melas are being conducted for bringing about settlements of disputes whether pending in Courts or outside.
  - In *Center of Legal Research v. State of Kerala,* AIR 1986 SC 2195, Justice Bhagwati observed "what is necessary is to supplement the traditional legal service programme with strategic legal service programme. It involves novel, radical, more dynamic and multi-dimensional uses of law and the legal process and seeks to provide representation to groups of social and economic protest."
- A common man has started feeling that justice itself is on trial. It is, therefore, imperative to evolve effective and efficient

strategies both preventive and protective: (1) To manage: Unmanageable; (2) To break: Unbreakable; (3) To beat: Unbeatable; (4) To hit: Unhittable; (5) To defend: Indefensible.

- In our country, amount spent or expenditure for administration of law and justice is reported 0.2 percent of the Gross Domestic Product (G.D.P.) which is grossly inadequate and insufficient in a democratic set up. It is, therefore, necessary to constitute a regular mechanism, whereby effective and ebullient reforms to translate this Constitutional mandate and obligation, a reality.
- *Legal literacy*- Legal literacy is a pre-condition to maintain the "rule of law". As observed by Justice Bhagwati, the strategic legal service consists of creating legal awareness or what may be described as promoting legal literacy, for knowledge of their rights and entitlement would give to the poor strength and confidence to fight and help them to avoid needless difficulties which arise from ignorance.
- The model scheme for Legal Aid evolved by the "Committee for Implementing Legal Aid Scheme (CILAS)" also included programme for promotion of legal literacy and spread of legal awareness among the weaker sections of the community by way of organizing legal Aid camps, especially in rural areas, slums or labour colonies.
- *PublicInterestLitigation*-Public Interest Litigation has been devised as a tool to secure benefit to a class or group of persons, either victims of exploitation, or oppression or who are denied the constitutional rights but cannot come to court personally for relief by reason of ignorance, poverty, destitution, helplessness, disability or social or economic disadvantage.
  - PIL is a form of litigation where jurisdiction of the Court is invoked on behalf of such

persons or group of persons by a third person or a social action group or a social organization regardless of its personal injury." The Supreme Court observed, "the poor too have civil and political rights and the Rule of Law meant for them also, though today it exists only on paper and not in reality" [People's Union for Democratic Rights v. Union of India, AIR 1982 SC 1473].

- For the first time the portals of the court are being thrown open to the poor and the downtrodden, the ignorant and the illiterate and their cases are coming before the Courts through public interest litigation which has been made possible by the judgment delivered by the Supreme Court in S.P. Gupta v. President of India, AIR 1982 SC 149 [Judges Appointment and Transfer case].
- In M.C. Mehta v. Union of India [AIR 1987 SC 1086], a constitutional Bench of the Apex Court while considering the scope of public interest litigation to grant compensation to the victims of hazardous or dangerous activities, has held that the law should keep pace with changing socio-economic norms; where a law of the past does not fit in the present context, the Court should evolve new law in a public interest litigation.
- In Bandhua Mukti Morcha v. Union of India [AIR 1984 SC 802, 815], the Supreme Court held that when the poor come before the Court, particularly for enforcement of their fundamental rights, it is necessary to depart from the adversarial procedure and to evolve a new procedure which will make it possible for the poor and the weak to bring the necessary material before the Court for the purpose of securing enforcement of their fundamental rights.

- The traditional rule in regard to 'locus standi' that judicial redress is available only to a person who has suffered a legal injury by reason of violation of his legal rights- by some agency or individual has now been considerably relaxed by the Supreme Court by the introduction of Public Interest Litigation.

The Institution of Lok Adalat

Lok Adalat has emerged lately as a new system of dispensation of justice and received tremendous response and wide support from different sections of the society. The system visualized as an alternative dispute settlement mechanism, evolved as a part of the CILAS programme with the object of taking justice to the doorsteps of the poor and to give speedy and cheap justice to those who cannot afford to fight the costly legal battle.

- ◦ *Lok Adalats or Niti Melas*- Lok Adalat has come to be seen as an institution or an agency, for handling disputes by conciliation and counseling, a species of peace making. Dispute in the Lok Adalats is resolved by discussion in an informal atmosphere, in which parties and panel members of the Lok Adalat participate, and settlement is reached with the mutual and free consent of the parties.
- ◦ Unlike in litigations concluded in our regular Courts, being in the nature of compromises, there is no winner and no loser in a mediated resolution of dispute by Lok Adalats. The intention being to help warring parties to work things out, shake hands, and become friends (or not enemies again), resolution of disputes in Lok Adalat, is more likely to bring or keep people together and, therefore, more conducive to harmonies.
- ◦ As part of CILAS programme, Lok adalats (Peoples' Courts) were constituted and niti melas were organized at various places in the country, under the supervision of State Legal Aid and Advice Boards, for the disposal, in a summary way and through the process of arbitration and settlement between the parties, of a large number of cases expeditiously and with lesser costs.
- ◦ The organizers of the Lok Adalats, fixed the date and place of the holding of Lok Adalats about a month in advance. Information about the holding of Lok Adalat was widely publicized through press and other means of publicity. Presiding Officers of various Courts were requested to look into the cases pending in their respective Courts and to see whether there was possibility of conciliation in these cases.
- ◦ Such of those cases where there was reasonable possibility of conciliation were identified and listed. Cases were analyzed, classified under various heads according to the nature of dispute and substance recorded. Then, pre-Lok Adalat conferences were held and parties to the dispute were approached and motivated by the legal aid teams, which included, law students, social workers and volunteers to resolve their disputes through Lok Adalats.
- ◦ Once parties had made a compromise or arrived at a settlement, it was reduced into writing by members of the panel of the Lok Adalat, signatures of the parties were obtained and countersigned by the members of the panel and passed on to the Court concerned for final decree or order.

- ◦ *Importance of the institution of Lok Adalat in the present context:* The revolutionary evolution of resolution of dispute by one or other means, Alternate Dispute Redressal (A.D.R.) mechanism, has been, successfully, translated in various countries. While, in India, roughly, 91 percent of cases instituted in the Courts go for trial and only 9 percent of cases are settled without judicial agitation, in U.S. A., more than 90 percent of cases involving legal disputes are settled before they go for trial.
- ◦ Most of the rural people in India who reside in more than 5,18,000 villages are either, illiterate, indigent or ignorant of their rights. Even in case of urban populace most of them are ignorant about their legal rights, who are otherwise, literate. The urbanized populace lack awareness about their legal rights. Our present traditional system of justice is suffering from maladies like huge and heavy expenses; unexpected and unpredictable delay in disposal and, cumbersome and complex process of Court.
- ◦ Pending workload of cases in Indian Courts has rapidly crossed the 30 millions as per latest survey, and many more are under inquiry or investigation stage, etc. The ratio of Judges per million in India is almost 9, whereas, it is more than 115 in U.S.A. In view of these circumstances, the institution of Lok Adalat is being looked upon as an effective Alternate Dispute

Redressal Forum, which has proved to be dialectical and speedy.

- *Legal status for Lok Adalat:* The Lok Adalat, a species of conciliatory agency, proved to be very popular in providing for a speedier system of administration of justice at lesser costs. The institution received wide support from concerned citizens and spread to disputes of diverse and varied nature and resolved cases pertaining to compoundable criminal complaints, civil and revenue disputes, MACT cases, and even institutional cases.
- *Public Participation in Legal Aid Programme- Role of Voluntary Organizations and Social Action Groups-* In *Centre of Legal Research* v. *State of Kerala,* AIR 1986 SC 2195, the Supreme Court held that there could be no doubt that if the legal aid programme was to succeed it must involve public participation. The court has emphasized the importance of role that could be played by voluntary organizations and social action groups in securing people's participation and involvement in the legal aid programme.
- *RoleoftheBenchandtheBar:*In various countries, particularly, in United States and other Western countries, the contribution of the Bar in rendering free and competent legal-aid is praiseworthy and it must be emulated. The Bar is, really, a backbone of the legal services to compliment and complete the Constitutional obligation and obtain statutory rights of millions of indigent, needy, handicapped and deserving people.

To save the Nation, a catalytic role has to be played by Legal Aid in the larger interest of weaker sections. N.A.L.S.A. has undertaken various important and effective and appreciable Legal-Aid programmes and, therefore, members of Bench and Bar, N.G.Os. and Government Agencies must render voluntary helping hand in such noble and novel projects.

* * * * *

The Legal Services Authorities Act, 1987

The Legal Services Authorities act, 1987 was enacted with a view to constitute Legal Services Authorities at National, State and District Levels which was brought into force with effect from 09-11-1995, almost eight years after its enactment. For the effective implementation of its schemes and to achieve the desired objective of providing Free Legal Aid and Advice to the poor, State Boards, District Legal Aid Committees and Taluk Committees were constituted under the LSA Act, 1987.

- Section-19. Organization of Lok Adalats- (1) Every State Authority or District Authority or the Supreme Court Legal Services Committee or every High Court Legal Services Committee or, as the case may be, Taluk Legal Services Committee may organize Lok Adalats at such intervals and places and for exercising such jurisdiction and for such areas as it thinks fit.
- Constitution of Lok Adalat- Every Lok Adalat organized for an area shall consist of such number of serving or retired judicial officers; and other persons, of the area as may be specified by the State Authority or the District Authority or the Supreme Court Legal Services Committee or the High Court Legal Services Committee, the Taluk Legal Services Committee, organizing such Lok Adalat. The experience and qualifications of other persons Lok Adalats shall be such as may be prescribed by the organizing authority.
- A Lok Adalat shall have jurisdiction to determine and to arrive at a compromise or settlement between the parties to a dispute in respect of any case pending before; or any matter, which is falling within the jurisdiction of, and is not brought before, any court for which the Lok Adalat is organized provided that the Lok Adalat shall have no jurisdiction in respect of any case or matter relating to an offence not compoundable under any law.

- Section-20- **Cognizance** of cases by Lok Adalats - Lok Adalat initiates proceedings when the parties thereof agree; or one of the parties thereof makes an application to the court, for referring the case to the Lok Adalat for settlement and if such court is prima facie satisfied that there are chances of such settlement or the matter is an appropriate one to be taken cognizance of by the Lok Adalat, the court shall refer the case to the Lok Adalat.
- When any such case is referred to a Lok Adalat, the Lok Adalat shall proceed to dispose of the case or matter and arrive at a compromise or settlement between the parties and shall be guided by the principles of justice, equity, fair play and other legal principles.
- Where no award is made by the Lok Adalat on the ground that no compromise or settlement could be arrived at between the parties, the record of the case shall be returned by it to the court, from which the reference has been received for disposal in accordance with law.

- Section-21- Award of Lok Adalat – Every award of the Lok Adalat shall be deemed to be a decree of a civil court or, as the case may be, an order of any other court and every award made by a Lok Adalat shall be final and binding on all the parties to the dispute, and no appeal shall lie to any court against the award.
- Section- 22. **Powers of Lok Adalats** -The Lok Adalat shall, for the purposes of holding any determination under this Act, have the same powers as are vested in a civil court under the Code of Civil Procedure, 1908 (5 of 1908) while trying a suit in respect of the following matters such as the power to summon and enforce the attendance of any witness and to examine him on oath, to order discovery and production of any document, to receive evidence on affidavits etc.
- All proceedings before a Lok Adalat shall be deemed to be judicial proceedings within the meaning of sections 193, 219 and 228 of the Indian Penal Code (45 of 1860) and every Lok Adalat shall be deemed to be a civil court for the purpose of section 195 and Chapter XXVI of the Code of Criminal Procedure, 1973 (2 of 1974).

Pre-Litigation Conciliation and Settlement of Disputes.

Chapter VI-A of the Legal Services authorities Act, 1987 provides for a scheme of Pre-Litigation Conciliation and Settlement of disputes. This system has been devised as a tool for amicable settlement of disputes before they reach courts.

- Section-22B. **Establishment of Permanent Lok Adalats** - (1) Notwithstanding anything contained in section 19, the Central Authority or, as the case may be, every State Authority shall, by notification, establish Permanent Lok Adalats at such places and for exercising such jurisdiction in respect of one or more public utility services and for such areas as may be specified in the notification.
- **Constitution of Lok Adalat or Permanent Lok Adalat-** It shall consist of a person who is, or has been, a district judge or additional district judge or has held judicial officer higher in rank than that of a district judge, who shall be the Chairman two other persons having adequate experience to be nominated by the Central or state Government as the case may be and the other terms and conditions of the appointment of the Chairman and other persons shall be such as may be prescribed by the Government.
- Section- 22C. **Cognizance of cases by Permanent Lok Adalat** - Any party to a dispute may, before the dispute is brought before any court, make an application to the Permanent Lok Adalat for the settlement of dispute.
- The Permanent Lok Adalat shall not have jurisdiction in respect of any matter relating to an offence not compoundable under any law and a matter in which the value of the property in dispute exceeds ten lakh rupees. However, the Central Government, may, by notification, increase the limit of ten lakh rupees in consultation with the Central Authority.

- On receiving statements, additional statements and reply, if any, filed by parties on the issues of the dispute, the Permanent Lok Adalat shall conduct conciliation proceedings between the parties to evolve an amicable settlement of the dispute in an independent and impartial manner guided by the principles of natural justice, objectivity, fair play, equity and other principles of justice, and shall not be bound by the Code of Civil Procedure, 1908 and the Indian Evidence Act, 1892.
- When a Permanent Lok Adalat, conciliation proceedings, is of opinion that there exists elements of settlement in such proceedings which may be acceptable to the parties, it may formulate the terms of a possible settlement and once the parties reach at an agreement on the settlement of the dispute, they shall sign the settlement agreement and the Permanent Lok Adalat shall pass an award in terms thereof and furnish a copy of the same to each of the parties concerned.
- Section- 22E- Award of Permanent Lok Adalat to be final- Every award of the Permanent Lok Adalat (on a majority of the persons constituting it), under this Act made either on merit or in terms of a settlement agreement shall be final and binding on all the parties thereto and on persons claiming under them and shall be deemed to be a decree of a civil court.
- Every award made by the Permanent Lok Adalat under this Act shall be final and shall not be called in question in any original suit, application or execution proceeding and the Permanent Lok Adalat may transmit any award made by it to a civil court having local jurisdiction and such civil court shall execute the order as if it were a decree made by that court.

It was observed by Justice Bhagwati in *Center of Legal Research v. State of Kerala*, AIR 1986 SC 2195 that "What is necessary is to supplement the traditional legal service programme with for the prevention and elimination of various kinds of injustices which the poor as a class suffer because of poverty and ignorance. It involves novel, radical, more dynamic and multi-dimensional uses of law and the legal process and seeks to provide representation to groups of social and economic protest." In this context, it could be concluded that Lok Adalats and schemes of Conciliation serve as a dynamic mechanism fo effective and amicable resolution of disputes so as to avoid the hassles of court proceedings and to avoid future enmity between parties to such disputes

******

Lok Adalat: A Mechanism of Alternate Dispute Resolution

(Abstract based on the writings of J.S. Bisht)

Introduction

The prevailing system of administration of justice based on the common law jurisprudence was found to be not suitable to the socio-economic conditions of this rural land and the formalism in law alienates the illiterate, destitute and deprived from the judicial process. Moreover, our justice delivery system is terribly expensive, dilatory and cumulatively disastrous. The result is that the legal system has lost its credibility for the weaker sections of the society. Justice has ever been the highest ideal of mankind and had been an urge behind all social upheavals and revolutions.

- The Concept of Equal Justice- Equal access to justice is the condition precedent for the claim and realization of the constitutional guarantee of justice-social, economic and political. Thus, "access to justice" is "a function of government in a civilized society to provide and maintain adequate and effective machinery, both within and outside the formal judicial process, to which all citizens, acting individually or as a group, can have access on an equal basis for the impartial resolution of their disputes".

- ◦ **Alternate Dispute Resolution Mechanism-** In the search for alternatives to the inherited model of adjudication through courts, litigants have come to adopt a variety of dispute settlement mechanisms, informal in approach, simple in techniques, speedy in process and cheap in administration. Among various ADR techniques negotiation, conciliation, mediation, arbitration etc. are commonly resorted to the world over for resolution of disputes.
- ◦ **Lok Adalat as an Effective ADR Tool-** Lok Adalat, being cheap, expeditious and indigenous, has acquired a pride of place in the hierarchy of various alternate dispute settlement mechanisms in the justice delivery system of India. "Lok Adalat concept and philosophy is an innovative Indian contribution to the world jurisprudence. It helps in emergence of jurisprudence of peace in the larger interest of justice and wider sections of society." In fact, amicable resolution of disputes is a sine qua non for social peace and harmony. Justice Khanna correctly observed that

"Judicial system is primarily intended to serve the needs of the community for providing justice with accountability, without which the people would move to the extra-judicial methods to settle the scores. If the people lose faith in the Bench and the Bar, they will easily take to remedies in the streets. This will inevitably lead to the downfall of democracy and the impotency of the court. The sense of injustice leads to frustration, which may in turn, compels the oppressed to rise against the system corroding the foundation of democracy and rule of law. History has numerous examples that even the mighty empires were vanished when they perpetrated injustice to their people."

Justice Brennon of the U. S. Supreme Court rightly observed that:

"Nothing rankles more in the human heart than a brooding sense of injustice. Illness we can put with. But injustice makes us pull the things down. When only the rich can enjoy the law, as a doubtful luxury, and the poor, who need it most, cannot have it because its expense puts it beyond their reach, the threat to the continued existence of free democracy is not imaginary but very real, because democracy's very life depends upon making the machinery of justice so effective that every citizen shall believe in and benefit by its impartiality and fairness."

- ◦ **Why Lok Adalats?-** The repeated maxim "Justice delayed is justice denied" comes true in view of the alarming backlog of pending cases before courts of different hierarchy resulting into dilatory justicing in India. This dismal situation compels the legislature and the judiciary to have an in-depth introspection about the deficiencies in our legal system and strongly advocates invoking the indigenous and traditional ADRs.
- ◦ The problem of back log of cases is not only peculiar to India but is a universal phenomenon. Sometimes the parties are not able to get justice in their life time and the new generation has to pursue the case in the quest of justice rendering the constitutional notion of equality and justice a teasing illusion to them. In this given state of affairs the mechanism of Lok Adalats is the only option left with the people to resort to for availing cheap and speedy justice.
- ◦ **Constitutional Mandate of Lok Adalats-** A government founded on anything except liberty and justice cannot stand. The Preamble of our Constitution makes it abundantly clear that justice -social, economic and political are the cherished object of our Constitution. The philosophy of equality before law has been deeply engrained in the scheme of our Constitution. Article 14 unequivocally states that, "The State shall not deny to any person equality before law or the equal protection of laws within the territory of India."
- ◦ The philosophy of equality can only be achieved when equal access to justice is ensured to the poor litigants by extending legal aid or through the mechanism of Lok Adalats. Article 38 of the Constitution advances the goal of social, economic and political justice, which mandates the State to secure a social order in which justice social, economic and political shall

inform all the institutions of the national life and to minimize inequalities in income and opportunities.

- To achieve the trilogy of justice as ordained in the Preamble of the Constitution, Article 39-A has been incorporated in the Constitution with an avowed intention that the State shall endeavor to secure that the operation of the legal system promotes justice on the basis of equal opportunities so that it is ensured that the opportunities for securing justices are not denied to any citizen by reason of economic or other disabilities.
- Judiciary was to be an arm of the social revolution, upholding the equality that Indians had longed for. And the higher judiciary being the sentinel of the Constitution is entrusted with the obligation to realize the constitutional goal of social justice. As

observed in *S.N.Patilv.MaheshYadav*, AIR 1987 SC 294, "modern judiciary could not obtain social legitimacy unit it interpreted law for socio-economic justice."

- **CILAs and Lok Adalats-** To realize the pledge of social justice in consonance with the spirit of Article 38 and 39-A of the Constitution legal aid schemes were formulated by constituting Legal Aid Boards at State level with the Committee for Implementation of Legal Aid Schemes at the apex under the Chairmanship of Justice P. N. Bhagwati to monitor and implement legal aid programmes on uniform basis in all the States and Union Territories of India. The efforts of CILAS and the popularity of Lok Adalats culminated in the enactment of the Legal Services Authorities Act, 1987, which conferred the statutory status of the Lok Adalats as an effective ADR for the resolution of pending and pre-trial litigation.
- **The Report on National Juridicare (Equal Justice-Social Justice-1977)-** This Report has specifically recommended particularly emphasizing on the establishment of Nyaya Panchayats and Lok Nyayalayas at the grass-root level for administering justice in the rural areas and on conciliations. The vigorous and resolute efforts of CILAS not only heralded the way for the legitimacy and popular acceptance of Lok Adalats but also constitutionalised and legalized the institution in the form of the Legal Services Authorities Act, 1987.
- **Statutory Foundation of Lok Adalats-** In pursuance of Article 39-A of the Constitution of India, the Parliament has enacted the Legal Services Authorities Act, 1987 with the legislative intent to constitute various legal services authorities to provide free and competent legal services to the weaker section of the society. The Act has conferred statutory status to Lok Adalats for the first time through the parliamentary legislation, although the institution had the glorious socio-cultural heritage in India. The significant feature of the Act is the incorporation of Chapter VI on Lok Adalats to organize them periodically within their jurisdiction.
- **Drawbacks of Lok Adalats-** The system of Lok Adalats envisaged under Chapter VI of the Act is based on compromise or settlement between the parties, therefore, jurisdiction exercised by the Lok Adalats is limited to making an effort by bringing about a settlement between the parties. The expression "to determine and arrive at a compromise or settlement" in sub-section (5) of Section 19 connotes that the Adalat can exercise the jurisdiction only when both the parties agree to arrive at a compromise or settlement. The moment one of the parties to the dispute expresses his unwillingness to arrive at a compromise or settlement, the Lok Adalat is denuded of its jurisdiction to deal with the matter in any manner.
- Thus, the consensus between the parties is indispensable for the functioning of the Adalats. And the failure on the part of the parties to arrive at a consensus, constraints the Adalats either to revert the matter back to the referring court or to advise the parties to seek remedy in a court of law, causing unnecessary delay in the dispensation of justice defeating the object of simple, cheap and speedy justice by relegating the parties back to the pre-reference stage.

- **Permanent Lok Adalats-** To overcome this major drawback in the existing scheme of Lok Adalats organized under Chapter VI of the Act that the new Chapter VI-A has been inserted in the Act by the Legal Services Authorities (Amendment} Act, 2002 to provide for the establishment of Permanent Lok Adalats for pre-litigation conciliation and settlement of disputes concerning Public Utility Services and to decide them on merits if no settlement is forthcoming.
- The PLA undertakes pretrial settlement on the application of any party to the dispute and subsequently other party is not allowed to invoke the jurisdiction of any court in the same dispute. On getting seized of the matter the PLA assists the parties to arrive at a settlement, where the parties does not reach the settlement, the PLA can decide the dispute on merits. However, while deciding the case on merits the PLAs shall be guided by the principles of justice, objectivity, fair play, equity and other principles of justice.
- **Anomalous Jurisdiction of PLAs-** The system of Lok Adalat is based on compromise and settlement. But the object sought to be achieved by the amended Act 37 of 2002 is contrary to the concept of Lok Adalat, for the failure of the parties to arrive at a compromise leads to compulsory adjudication by creating a bar on seeking other remedies available under law by locking the parties within the indomitable adjudicatory precincts of the PLAs.
- Moreover, the jurisdiction of PLAs and Consumer Forums constituted under the Consumer Protection Act, 1986 are identical in respect of the Public Utility Services and the amendment has considerably whittled down the jurisdiction of the Consumer Forums to the barest minimum.
- Section 22E (1) of the Act makes the award of the PLA final and binding, whether made as a result of settlement or on merits. The provision by taking away the power or judicial review of the courts, subverts the basic structure of the Constitution of India. Whereas, in consonance with the theory of basic structure the apex court has held categorically that judicial review of the courts cannot be taken away by any law, therefore, violates the basic premise of the Constitution.
  - **Functioning Of Lok Adalats-** Lok Adalats resolve compoundable offences, motor vehicle claims, labour disputes, matrimonial and family disputes, bank loans, insurance claims and such other matters. The disposal statistics speaks volumes of the success and popularity of the institution and "it is expected that very soon a large number of disputes between public and statutory authorities would start getting settled at pre- litigation stage itself saving the parties from unnecessary expense and litigational inconvenience".
- The mechanism of Lok Adalats has contributed significantly in reducing the backlog of cases pending in subordinate judiciary and can equally relieve the higher judiciary from incoming litigation in the form of appeal, revision etc. by settling the dispute finally once for all.
- The Law Commission of India, 129th Report on Urban Litigation-Mediation as Alternative to Adjudication, 1988 observed that "Lawyers can be a potential wing of the Lok Adalat justice delivery system but the present legislative scheme has made it to breathe at a

distance from the legal profession, hijacking their traditional role in isolation of lawyers but in a manner enjoying their active confidence.

- However, the plight of poor litigants approaching Lok Adalats through the bastion of legal aid is quite deplorable. Lamenting on the poor quality of legal service extended under the rubric of legal aid the Supreme Court held that "right to defend includes right to effective and meaningful defence". To ensure quality legal assistance the Court directed the State to fix better remuneration for lawyers, stressing that legal aid through a raw talent amounts to denial of legal aid and hits the equality clause of Article 14 of our Constitution.

CONCLUSION

Conciliatory justice is said to be able to produce qualitative better results than contentious litigation which often results in final break of the relationship among the litigants. The adopted procedure is more accessible, more rapid, informal, less expensive and the adjudicators are more capable and eager to understand the parties' plight and the environment in which it has arisen. The institution of Lok Adalat has been embraced by the people as a mechanism of ADR, which has the potential to support the judicial process in the resolution of the disputes amicably.

At the reference stage the court should give patient hearing to the parties to explore the possibilities of settlement on fair terms and to remove the apprehension from their minds. In

majority of the cases government is a party, therefore, the availability of the administrative

officers for participating in the conciliation process must be ensured. Unless and until the government adopts a positive and pragmatic attitude towards Lok Adalats, there will be difficulties and constraints in the functional future of the institution. Social workers must participate actively with the judicial officers in the proceedings and they should be given orientation in the amicable dispute resolution techniques.

The Amendment Act establishing Permanent Lok Adalats for pre- trial settlement of disputes concerning the Public Utility Services and to decide them on merits on failure of the parties to arrive at a settlement is not a welcome measure, since it is contrary to the concept and spirit of the Lok Adalat. Instead of the establishment of PLAs the existing scheme of Lok Adalats should have been strengthened by increasing the frequency in their organization and empowering them with pre-trial settlement of disputes.

The institution of Lok Adalats is a welcome measure since it eliminates the possibilities of long drawn litigation by way of appeal or revision and relieves the parties from getting the briefs prepared, procuring witnesses and attending the court and lawyer's chambers without certainty of adjudication. The solution should be practicable and in consonance with the rights and duties of the parties. The popularity, functioning and acceptance of the institution hold a great promise in bringing down the backlog of arrears and promoting the cause of social justice.

*****

Legal Profession and the Advocates Act, 1961

(Abstract of the writings of *A.N. Veera Raghvan*, edited by *H S Bhalla*)

- **King's Courts**- Law, as a profession, appears to have been in vogue in ancient Indian thought. Its concept was quite different from that it is today pursuant to the **Regulating Act of 1773**, authorized by the King's Charter of Letters Patent, the Supreme Court, was established at Fort William in Bengal through a Charter issued on the 26th of March, 1774.
- The Advocates' entitled to appeal were only the English and Irish barristers and members of the Faculty of 5 Advocates in Scotland; the attorneys referred to were the Irish attorneys and solicitors. The Court was thus an exclusive preserve for member of the British legal profession. An Indian lawyer had no right of appearance in the Courts.
- **Company's Courts**- Prior to the rise of British power in India, in Northern India, Justice was administered by Courts established by the Mughal Emperors and legal representatives called Vakils were available to litigants in these native Courts.
- **The Bengal Regulation VII of 1793** created for the first time a regular legal profession for the Company's Courts. The Bengal Regulation regulated the appointment of Vakils or native pleaders in the Courts of Civil judicature in the provinces of Bengal, Bihar and Orissa and only Hindus and Muslims could be pleaders.

- Under the **Bengal Regulation XXVII of 1814**, pleaders were empowered to act as arbitrators and give legal opinions on payment of fees. The next important legislation was the **Bengal Regulation XII of 1833** which introduced a change. In that only persons duly qualified, to whatever nationality or religion they might belong would be enrolled as pleaders of the Sadar Dewani Adalat.
- **The Bengal Practitioners Act, 1846,** made three important changes namely;

1. The office of pleaders was thrown open to all persons of whatever nationality by the Sadar Courts to be of good character and duly qualified for the office.
2. Attorneys and barristers of any of Her Majesty's Courts in India were eligible to plead in any of the Sadar Courts subjects to the rules of those Courts as regards language or otherwise.
3. The pleaders were permitted to enter into agreements with their clients for their fees for professional services.

- **The Legal Practitioners Act, 1855,** permitted also barristers and attorneys of the Supreme Court not entitled till then to be admitted as pleaders in the Courts of the East India Company.
- The position clearly underwent a change after the British Crown took over the administration of the country from the Company and the **Government of India Act, 1858,** was passed. **The Indian High Courts Act, 1862** was enacted by the British Parliament authorizing the setting up by Letters Patent of High Courts in the several presidencies.

- Clause 9 of the *Letters* Patent of 1865 which replaced the earlier Letter Patent creating a High Court in Calcutta authorized it to approve, admit and enroll advocates, Vakils and attorneys.
- **The Legal Practitioners Act, 1879-** The Legal Practitioners Act, 1879 was enacted to consolidate and amend the Law relating to legal practitioners of the High Courts. The Attorneys were under the disciplinary jurisdiction of the High Courts under this Act. Section 4 of the Act empowered an advocate or Vakil on the roll of any High Court, or any Court in British India.
- The Chartered High Courts rules had been framed putting the requirement for admission of the Vakil a graduate in Arts or Science, taken a degree in law and served as an articled Clerk with a Vakil of five years' standing.
- Under section 6 of the Act of 1879, High Courts were given the power to make rules as to the qualifications, admissions, and certificates of proper persons to be:

a. Pleaders of the subordinate Courts and of the revenue offices and;
b. To be mukhtars of subordinate courts, and the fees to be paid for the examination and admission of such persons.

- **The Legal Practitioners (women) Act, 1923-** This Act was passed specially providing that notwithstanding anything contained in the previous enactments or other provisions in this regard, "no Women shall, by reason only of her sex, be disqualified from being admitted or enrolled as a legal practitioner" examination.
- Section 27 of the 1923 Act empowered the High Court to fix and regulate from time to time the fees payable by any party in respect of his adversary's advocate, pleader, Vakil, mukhtar or attorney.
- **The Chamber Committee and the Indian Bar Councils Act, 1926-** Dissatisfaction was expressed about the distinction that existed- between barristers and Vakil, and the special privileges enjoyed by the British barristers and solicitors. Consequently, the Government of India had to constitute in November, 1923, the Indian Bar Committee known as the Chamber Committee to report on:

i. The proposals made from time to time for constitution of Indian Bar, whether on all India or provincial basis, with particular reference to the constitution, statutory recognition, functions and authority of a Bar Council or Bar Councils, and their positions, vis- à-vis High Courts.

ii. The extent to which it might be possible to remove the distinction enforced by statute of practice between barristers and Vakils.

- **The Bar Councils Act, 1926-** This Act was passed with a view mainly to implement some of the recommendations of the Chamber Committee and to consolidate and amend the law, relating to the legal practitioners. Consequently, Bar Councils were constituted in the different provinces on different dates in and after 1928.
- The Act of 1926 introduced some changes. Every Bar Council was to comprise of fifteen members, with the Advocate General as an ex-officio member, and four members

nominated by the High Court, and ten members elected by and from amongst advocates of the High Court. The term of the Bar Council was for a period of three years.

- According to the 1926 Act, the High Court had to prepare and maintain a roll of advocates, Vakils and pleaders entitled as of right to practice immediately before the date when sanction of the Act was brought into force and of all and others admitted thereafter as advocates.
- Section 9 of the Bar Councils Act, authorized the Bar Council, with the sanction of the High Court to make rules to regulate the admission of persons to be advocates, to prescribe the qualifications of persons applying for admission as advocates, to regulate the admission as advocates.
- The qualifications for admission as laid down under the rules permitted those who had taken a degree in law and barristers and attorneys to be enrolled. An applicant for enrolment had to pay a stamp duty for the entry in the rolls as provided for under the Indian Stamp Act.
- Section 14 of the Act empowered an advocate to practice: -

i. In the High Court where he was enrolled, subject to the rules.
ii. In all subordinate Courts and tribunals.

- It may be pointed out that under the Act of 1926, the power of enrolment of advocates virtually remained in the High Court. The function of the Bar Council was advisory in nature. The right of the advocates of one High Court to practice in another High Court was made subject to the rules made by the, High Court.
- **The recommendations of an India Bar Committee and the Law Commission-** With the coming into force of the Constitution in 1950 and the establishment of a Supreme Court for India the need for an all-India bar was stressed by the legal fraternity. In this situation, the Union Government set up a Committee known as the All India Bar Committee under the Chairmanship of Justice S.R. Das of the Supreme Court.
- Subsequently in 1955 the Law Commission, presided over by Mr. M.C. Stelvad, then Attorney-General of India, in its fourteenth report on the Reform of Judicial Administration endorsed the recommendations of the All India Bar Committee, as regard the creation of a unified All India Bar as well as the establishment, composition and functions of the State and all India Bar Councils.
- To implement these recommendations, the Legal Practitioners Bill, 1959, was introduced in the Lok Sabha on 19th November, 1959. When the Bill came to be passed, the name legal Practitioners Bill was changed into the Advocate Act.
- **The Advocates Act, 1961,** which received the assent of the President of India on the 18th May, 1961, extends to the whole of India, except the State of Jammu and Kashmir. Broadly speaking, the main features of the Act are:

I. to have, in course of time only one class of legal practitioners viz. advocates,

II. to take away the powers till then vested in the Courts, in the matter of admission of advocates and the maintenance of the rolls, and their disciplinary, and

III. to constitute a Central Bar Council with powers, inter alia, to recognize the degree in law for admission as advocates.

- Every State Bar Council consists of- (i) the Advocate-General as the ex-officio member (for the Bar Council of Delhi, since there is no Advocate-General for the Union Territory of Delhi, the Additional Solicitor General was made the ex-officio member, and when the office was made the ex-officio member, and when the office was abolished, the Solicitor-General of India was made ex- officio members, and

- (ii) in the case of the Bar Councils of Assam and Nagaland, Orissa, Delhi and Himachal Pradesh fifteen other members and in the case of all the other State Bar Councils twenty other members elected in accordance with the system of proportional representation by means of the single transferable vote from amongst the advocates on the electorate of the State Bar Council concerned.

- The Act as originally passed prescribed a term of six years for an elected member of a State Bar Council subject to the principle of rotation but this provision has since been amended and the term as now fixed is four years from the date of the publication of the result of the election.

- Every State Bar Council has- one or more disciplinary Committee, an executive Committee, consisting of five members, an enrolment Committee, consisting of those members and each other Committees as may be deemed necessary. Each Bar Council has a Chairman and a Vice-Chairman elected in such manner as may be prescribed and has to appoint Secretary, and an accountant, if necessary.

- The functions of a State Bar Council are to admit persons as advocates on its roll, to prepare and maintain such roll, to entertain and determine cases of misconduct against advocates on its roll; to safeguard the rights privileges and interests of advocates on its roll, to promote and support law reform; to provide for the Election of its members; to perform all other functions assigned to it by or under the Act and to do all other things necessary for discharging the aforesaid functions.

- The Bar Council of India: Membership and Function- The Act provides that there shall be a Bar Council known as the Bar Council of India, which consists of the Attorney General of India, and the Solicitor-General of India as ex-officio members, and one member elected by each State Bar Council from amongst its members. There shall be a Chairman and a Vice-Chairman of the Bar Council of India elected as prescribed by rules and a Secretary, and an Accountant, if any, under Section 7.

- The functions of the Bar Council of India are to prepare and maintain a common roll of advocates, to lay down standards of professional conduct and etiquette for advocates, to lay down the procedure to be followed by its disciplinary committee of each State Bar Council; to safeguard the rights; privileges and interests, of advocates; to promote and support law reform; to deal with and dispose of any matter arising under Act, which may

be referred to it by a State Bar Council to exercise general supervision and control over State Bar Councils.

- Further, the BCI is to promote legal education and to lay down standards of such education, in consultation with the Universities whose degree in law shall be a qualification for enrolment of an advocate and for the purpose visit and inspect Universities; to manage and invest the funds of the Bar Council, to provide for the election of its members; to perform all other functions conferred on it by or under the Act and to all other thing necessary for discharging the aforesaid functions.

- The Bar Council of India is to have one or more disciplinary Committee, a Legal Education Committee, an executive Committee, and such other Committees as may be deemed necessary. The main source of income of the Bar Council of India is out of the fee paid by each applicant for enrolment to the State Bar Council.

- Senior Advocates- Persons who were "senior advocates immediately before the appointed day, i.e. 1-12-1961 have been deemed to be senior advocates for the purpose of the Act. Besides, power has been conferred under Section 16 of the Act to the Supreme Court and the High Courts to designate any advocate as senior advocate if in its opinion by virtue of his ability, experience and standing at the Bar, he is deserving of such distinction.

- **Qualifications, for admission as an advocate-** Section 24 of the Act lays down the qualification for admission as an advocate namely:

i. A person who has obtained a degree in law from any University in India or from any University outside the territory of India, recognized by the Bar Council of India for the purposes of the Act,

ii. A barrister;

iii. A Vakil or a Pleader who is a law graduate if his application for enrolment was made within two years from the appointed day viz. 1-12-1961;

iv. A person who has for at least three years been a vakil or a pleader or a mukhtar or was at any time entitled to be enrolled under any law for the time being in force as an advocate of a High Court or of a Court of a Judicial Commissioner or in any Union Territory.

- An applicant for admission has to be a citizen of India and should have completed the age of 21 years. He should pay the required fee to the State Bar Council and should fulfill the other requirement as laid down by the rules of the State Bar Councils.

- **Legal Qualifications-** A person to be eligible to join the course of study in law should be a graduate of University or hold such academic qualification which is considered by the Bar Council of India equivalent to a graduate degree of a University. During the last year of the course, the instruction and practical training should also be imparted for a period of six months in the rules of courts and in drafting and pleadings and documents.

- According to the resolution of the Bar Council of India, practical training would include pleading and conveyancing, moot courts and conducting civil and criminal proceedings, attending courts; maintaining a record of the above three requirements and arrangements of at least six lectures of professional ethics, attendance at four of which shall be compulsory.

- The rules on standards of legal education were made, as required under the Act, in consultation with the Universities imparting legal education and the State Bar Councils. In accordance with the above rules, the Bar Council of India in exercise of the powers to visit and inspect Universities, imparting legal education.

- **Conditions for admissions to roll-** Section 28 of the Act empowers the State Bar Councils to make rules, subject to the approval of the Bar Council of India. The rules can be made on the conditions subject to which a person may be admitted as an advocate on the roll of Bar Council. The rules accordingly made by State Bar Councils generally prohibit the enrolment of a person who though he may be otherwise qualified,, is in full or part time service or employment or is engaged in any trade or profession.

- The prohibition against enrolment does not apply to certain categories of persons specifically referred to in the proviso to the rule such as 'law officers' fulfilling certain conditions, articled clerk or an attorney, a person in part-time service as a professor or Lecturer, teacher in law of a person who by virtue of his being a member of a Hindu Joint Family has an interest in a Joint management thereof or other classes of persons specifically exempted after approval by the Bar Council of India.

- The compulsory subjects are: Indian Legal and Constitutional History, Contracts, Torts, Family Law including Hindu and Mohammedan Law; Evidence, Legal Theory (Jurisprudence and Comparative Law): Civil Procedure, Limitation and Arbitration.

- **Application for admission to roll-** An application for admission as an advocate has to be made in the prescribed form to the State Bar Council within whose jurisdiction the applicant proposes to practice. If the enrolment committee proposed to refuse such applications, it has to refer the application with the statement of the grounds in support of the refusal to the Bar Council of India, and has to dispose of the application finally in conformity with such opinion.

- **Right to practice**- Chapter IV Section 29 of the Advocates Act regulates the right of Advocate to practice throughout the territories through which the Act extends in all courts including the Supreme Court, before any tribunal or person legally authorized to take evidence of before any other authority or person before whom such advocate is entitled to practice. Further, under Section 33 advocates alone are entitled to practice in any Court.
- **Practice by persons not entitled to practice**- Persons illegally practicing in Courts or before other authorities when they are not entitled to practice under the provisions of the Act are liable for punishment with imprisonment for a term which may extend to six months.

- **Some important powers of the Bar Council or India**- Apart from the other powers already enumerated the Bar Council of India has been specifically conferred certain special powers namely;

  1. **Power to remove name from the rolls**-The Bar Council of India is empowered, to remove an enrolled person from the roll of advocates after giving him an opportunity of being heard by way of punishment for misconduct in disciplinary proceedings.
  2. **Revision**- The Bar Council of India has the power at any time to call for the record of any proceedings under the Act, which has been disposed of by a State Bar Council or a Committee thereof, and from which no appeal lies, for satisfying itself as to the legality or propriety of such a disposal and may pass such orders thereon as it deemed fit.
  3. **Directives**- Section 48 B empowers the Bar Council India for the proper and efficient discharge of the functions of a State Bar Council or any committee thereof, to give such directions to the State Bar Council or its committees as may appear it to be necessary, and the State Bar Council or the Committee has to comply with the directions.
  4. **Rules 'to make rules and approval'**- Section 15 enumerates

the powers of the State Bar Councils and the Bar Council of India to make rules on the matters dealt with Chapter II of the Act relating to the Bar Councils. Further, any rule made by State Bar Council, whether under Section 15 or 28 shall have effect only if it has been approved by the Bar Council of India. Section 49 confers on the Bar Council of India a general power to make rules for discharging its functions under the Act.

- **Supreme Court Rules to regulate the legal profession**- Prior to the coming into force of the Constitution, the Federal Court was empowered under Section 214 of the Government of India Act, 1935 to make rules, with the approval of the Governor General, for regulating the practice and procedure of the Court including rules as to the persons practicing before it.
- Article 145(1) of the Constitution empowers the Supreme Court to make rules, with the approval of the President inter alia as to persons practicing before it. The Supreme Court Rules, 1950 made in exercise of powers under Article 145(1) provides for the enrolment of persons as advocates who are entitled to practice before it.
- Order IV of the Supreme Court Rules deals with the Advocates. Rule 2(b) places some restrictions on the senior advocates. Rule 3 provides that every advocate appearing before the court shall wear robes and costumes as may from time to time be directed by the Court. In pursuance of this rule the Chief Justice of India directed that the costume that be worn by the advocates appearing before the Supreme Court should be black coat, robe and band worn by the barristers appearing before the High Courts.

- Rule 5 lays down that an advocate shall not be qualified to be registered as an advocate on record unless he has undergone training for one year with an advocate on record approved by the Court and has thereafter passed such tests as may be held by the Court for advocates who apply to be registered as advocates on record.
- The Supreme Court Advocate (Practice in High Court) Act, 1951, conferred the right on every advocate of the Supreme Court, to practice in any High Court whether or not he is an advocate of that High Court. In *Aswani Kumar Ghosh v. Arabindha Ghosh*, the Supreme Court held that an advocate of the Supreme Court became entitled as of right to appear

and plead as well as act in all the High Courts in India.

CONCLUSION

What has been enumerated above will show that the Advocates Act. 1961, has marked the beginning of a new era in the history of the legal profession by vesting largely in the Bar Councils the power and the jurisdiction which the Courts till then exercised, by fulfilling the aspirations of those who had been demanding an all Indian Bar and effecting a unification of the Bar in India, power to practice in all the Courts and bound by rules made and code of conduct laid down by their own bodies to which the members of Council resort to for the protection of their rights, interests or privileges. The Act has enabled representatives from the several States to come together to a common forum, and has brought about integration.

The conferment of the power in respect of legal education and the recognition of the

degree in law and the power to visit and inspect universities imparting legal education, have

resulted in a uniform pattern of legal education, while at the same time preserving intact the powers and responsibilities of the universities. A word of caution is necessary at this stage. The problem of language in so far at any rate as regards legal education might present difficulties and would seem to be of utmost magnitude. This would require defect less handling.

An attempt had been made to provide by legislation for the Attorney-General of India to be the ex-officio Chairman of the Bar Council of India and for the Advocate-General in the States to be the Chairman of the Bar Councils. But this had been stoutly resisted by the Bar Councils, on the ground that it would encroach upon the autonomy given to the Bar Councils. As a result the Government had to drop the matter.

****

Contents